S0-AHF-848

THE CHURCH
BETWEEN TEMPLE AND MOSQUE

140257

BR
127
.B35

The Church Between Temple and Mosque

A STUDY OF THE RELATIONSHIP BETWEEN THE CHRISTIAN FAITH AND OTHER RELIGIONS

by

J. H. BAVINCK

BIP=95

WILLIAM B. EERDMANS PUBLISHING COMPANY
GRAND RAPIDS, MICHIGAN

GOSHEN COLLEGE LIBRARY
GOSHEN, INDIANA

after 1965

Copyright © by William B. Eerdmans Publishing Co.
All rights reserved.
Library of Congress Catalog Card Number, 66-22946.
Printed in the United States of America.

PREFACE

This posthumous work of a much loved and highly esteemed missiologist clearly illumines the right stance of Christians in dialogue with persons of other faiths. Its simplicity and profundity make it appealing to the serious layman; to missionary, evangelist, and pastor; and to the scholar. These chapters were originally lectures given to a small class of students in an American university, and they still have the tone of a superb teacher's quiet, intimate talking with concerned, inquiring hearers. This quality makes the book unusually well adapted to the understanding of serious readers who are for the first time approaching this weighty, urgent problem of the relation of Christianity to other religions and what it is to which Christians can testify. It takes them into the heart of other faiths as well as their own. A lifetime of scholarship and of missionary encounter with men of other religions, on the one hand, and a warm, sure personal faith in the Gospel, on the other, have been distilled into the pages of this book.

Towards the end of the book Professor Bavinck states that, standing between temple and mosque, the Church cannot avoid dialogue with them. It is not enough for the Church merely to witness. "It has the duty to speak honestly and with dignity with the other religions." The author shows where the Christian stands both in community with, and over against, other religions. That same irenic, understanding, appreciative

5

spirit which made the writer of the book so effective a mediator and bridge-builder between Christians of divergent views, is here manifested again in the encounter between differing faiths. But sympathy and understanding do not add up to syncretism. Confessing his own sins of repression of God's truth and will, humbly and without pride the disciple of Christ must assert: "God is different, totally different, from the way we humans have imagined Him in our religious fantasies. In Jesus Christ alone, the *Logos,* the Word, we hear His voice and see His image."

Dialogue is possible because of the common sharing in the universal religious consciousness among men and because of the reality of general revelation or the work of God among all peoples and all religions. The antagonisms and tensions, the often opposing polarities, within this religious consciousness are honestly exposed; but with equal clarity the author describes the "five magnetic points" which have drawn the attention of men and provide the common ground. The second part of the book is an attempt to listen to God's Word on the major issues, through reflection on Romans, chapter 1. In the light of what he hears spoken out of the Bible the Christian can then speak on these subjects in dialogue, and not in disputation, with persons of other faiths. Many a reader will finally put this book down with a new understanding of many aspects of the Gospel.

This last book by Professor Bavinck is undoubtedly "to the furtherance of [that] Gospel."

—R. PIERCE BEAVER

CONTENTS

INTRODUCTION

CHAPTER I

THE CHRISTIAN FAITH AND OTHER RELIGIONS

The subject we are discussing here is a very old one. The relationship between the Christian faith and other religions was already discussed when the Christian Church was no more than a small group, scattered over the whole Roman Empire, despised, persecuted, and living in very difficult circumstances. Even in that time some Christians ventured to say something about this intriguing problem — remarkable words, sometimes, which today are still not forgotten, and still continue to play a part in the discussions of our time. Later on, when the Christian Church had spread over large parts of Europe and was preoccupied with itself, its confession, and organization, this matter had lost its urgency and was gradually pushed aside. Still, it was never lost sight of altogether, for it remained in the background of the history of the Church as a strange riddle. It was only waiting for the time when it would get a new chance to come to the fore.

And now this new chance has come. It had, in fact, already

come when the Moslem armies began to threaten the Western world. It came again when the Pope sent missionaries to remote parts of the globe, to the Chinese empire far away in the East, to India, and to other countries. And it received new and overwhelming impetus when colonial empires were formed, when ships from Portugal, Spain, England and the Netherlands discovered islands and continents, the existence of which had previously been unknown. In those days, especially, this problem arose anew and demanded serious consideration. Missionaries suddenly were compelled to wrestle with it. They had gone to other countries to preach the gospel, but they could not prevent adherents of other religions from asking them questions. Somehow they had to give an answer to these questions. They had to make it clear in which respects the teachings of Buddha or of Mohammed were different from the gospel. They were compelled to enter deeply into the problem of the relationship between the Christian faith and other religions.

It is certain that this problem has never been so urgent as in our own day. Today there are churches in almost every mission field in the world. These churches exist amidst millions of people who adhere to religions other than Christianity and who put their trust in other prophets. For those churches it is impossible to avoid discussion with the leaders and priests of non-Christian communities. The very existence of these churches is at stake. Their leaders have to reply to the indictments of their fellow countrymen, because they live with them in the same cities and country. It is no wonder that in our day the churches in India, China, and the Moslem countries search and seek with great intensity, studying and discussing that very old problem which is nevertheless new in every age. So let us join them in their investigations and deliberations, because we see the immense importance of their fierce struggle. Together we shall try to find an answer to the problem of the relationship between the Christian faith and other religions.

PRELIMINARY CONSIDERATIONS

First of all, we must look at our subject more closely and more thoroughly. What are we aiming at when we intend to speak of the Christian faith and other religions? As soon as we begin to tackle our subject, it strikes us that an answer is already given, even though vaguely. It is important to scrutinize that answer, nebulous though it may be.

The answer which lies concealed in our subject appears to be of an ambivalent character. It suggests that the Christian faith and those other religions have something in common, of course they have! A Christian who is accustomed to pray cannot help recognizing that the Moslem whom he sees praying is doing something similar. And seeing a Hindu bowing down before his god stirs the Christian, because he himself has learned to bow his head before the God who appeared to us in Jesus Christ. Indeed, he cannot deny that our Christian faith and those other religions have something in common, that there are certain similarities between them. The word *other* actually puts it very clearly: the Christian faith is also a religion. When we list the great world religions, we must mention the Christian faith alongside the others.

This simple fact has a deeper meaning than we may be inclined to admit. It means that Christianity and the other religions are somehow comparable. This does not mean, of course, that there are not also great differences. The republic of Andorra, and the United States, are both independent nations, and so they belong to the same category, although they greatly differ in size, economic power, and political prestige. But the resemblance between the Christian faith and other religions has more far-reaching consequences, one of which is that the Bible can be translated into every language and can be understood by all people of every language. There are words which can be used for God, the Creator of heaven and earth, or for sin or for salvation. It hardly needs to be said that each of these words which we borrow from other languages is infected with non-Christian concepts. In the context of the religions

which have put their mark upon these languages these words
have an entirely different meaning — their god is different
from the Father of our Lord Jesus Christ, their idea of sin is
wholly unlike the biblical concept of it. Nevertheless it is of
extreme importance that these words exist, and that we can
use them. The preacher of the gospel who makes a serious
effort to express the substance of his message in one of these
languages has to be very careful. He must be aware of the
fact that in employing the terms of that language he runs the
risk of being completely misunderstood, because his audience
inevitably hears in each term connotations which are different
from what he has in mind. And yet he will feel very thankful
that he *can* apply them. His situation would have been much
worse, and much more hopeless, had he been confronted with
nothing but an immense mental void. Then communication
would have been utterly impossible.

Here we already touch upon the second suggestion hinted at
in our subject. When we are dealing with Christianity and
other religions we silently assume that, notwithstanding the fact
that they are comparable, there exists a deep gulf between them.
Although the Christian faith is one of several different religions,
this does by no means imply that they are more or less identical
and rooted in the same soil. Our subject suggests at least the
possibility that they are radically different. When we compare the United States of America and the republic of Andorra,
we see that there is a great quantitative difference between
these two countries. But when we compare religions we find
that quantity does not mean a great deal. What we are confronted with are *qualitative* differences, differences which cannot
easily be fathomed because they originate from a difference
in background. The Christian faith claims that it is something
entirely different and of a unique character.

In our investigations we shall try to find out whether this
claim is legitimate, and justifiable by the facts. It is clear that
this will not be an easy task; it might even prove to be an
impossible undertaking. Is not one of the most essential fea-

tures of every religion that it demands a personal decision, and that such a decision is always a matter of faith? Philosophical reasoning does not take us very far when we are dealing with phenomena that are urged by the heart rather than by sophisticated deliberations. Nevertheless we cannot avoid the necessity of giving an answer to the question: What does the Christian faith mean when it claims to be unique?

Before we can begin this examination, however, there are still other points which need further clarification, for otherwise we will constantly be in danger of becoming bogged down in a multitude of side-issues.

The first point we have to discuss is the meaning of the word *religion*. We have already used it many times, and in the course of our discussion we shall, quite naturally, have to make use of it on almost every page. But what does this word mean? What is the origin and the essence of religion, and which are the basic characteristics of it? As soon as we reflect on this problem we see that we shall have to make a choice between two possibilities.

The first possibility is that religion belongs to the nature and structure of man. The history of mankind shows very clearly that man is gifted with a variety of aptitudes and capabilities. Man is a thinker, a dreamer; he naturally wrestles with the riddles of the mysterious world in which he finds himself. Man is a technician; he likes to invent new gadgets which make life more comfortable and worthwhile. Man is an artist; he is born with a sense of music and beauty. Man is endowed with a sense of humor; he is, in fact, the only creature that can laugh. And among all those inclinations and capabilities we find that man is obviously a religious being. He cannot help being religious. He himself cannot account for it, nor does he have the vaguest inkling of where it comes from, but apparently his being religious belongs to the equipment which nature has given him, and that is why we find religion everywhere in the world. Even when a man turns his back upon the religious traditions in which he has been brought up and calls himself an atheist, he still remains in the grasp of his religious predisposition. He can never wholly rid himself of it.

Of course this is not to say that every man has this religious trait to the same extent. Man has a sense of music, but not every man has it to the same degree. This also applies to man's religiousness. Among every people there are men and women in whose life religion seems to be the only important and dominating thing. But there are also men and women who only rarely show themselves to be religious in the real sense of the word. Apparently there is a variety of inclinations and aptitudes, but it cannot be denied that religiousness is proper to man.

It stands to reason that many philosophers in ancient as well as in modern times have paid attention to the unavoidable question of the origin and essence of religion. Some of them have assumed that our religiousness is somehow connected with our being reasonable creatures. Man is a thinker and a philosopher. That means that when he encounters problems and mysteries he is always busy trying to find the answers to them. He wants to know where this world came from; he is interested in the primeval cause of everything. He is not content to live, to love and to die; he wants to find out why everything is as it is, and to understand the purpose of his life. And all those questions with which he struggles make him realize that there was a god, or that there were gods, who built this wonderful palace which we call the world. Thus he is a religious creature — because he is a reasonable creature.

The great German philosopher Immanuel Kant defended the idea that religion is rooted in our awareness of our moral responsibility. During our life on earth we are confronted repeatedly with the mysterious "ought," with the "categorical imperative," which commands us to do what is morally justifiable. Man may try to excuse himself and to escape from the tyranny of this severe master, but he never succeeds in silencing this accusing voice. His religion is the result of the acknowledgment of his responsibility.

Others have emphasized that religion has something to do with our emotional character. We are religious because we are able to realize that the universe is great and that we are dependent on powers which are immensely greater than we are. In all these conceptions, different though they may be, it is taken for granted that religion is an element in human nature. Man's religiousness is a quality which belongs to the structure of his being. Here and there the suggestion has been made that religiousness is characteristic only of man as long as he lives in a state of primitiveness and immaturity. Primitive man is naturally religious, therefore, because for him the world is not primarily an "it" but a "thou." He believes that the forces of nature are gods or spirits which intentionally favor him or hurt him. His relationship to nature is a reciprocal one; in his naive imagination he supposes that this amazing world is full of both friendly and hostile powers. This view holds that modern man does not need religion any more, because his eyes have already been opened and he has reached the state of maturity. Religiousness is not in the same sense a quality of man's nature as are his being a thinker and being susceptible to beauty. The latter are ineradicable, and will never vanish; but his being religious is characteristic of him only during a certain period of his development.

In recent times an even more pernicious verdict has been given on religion. Freudian psychology put forward the hypothesis that religion is a neurotic disease. The god whom we adore, on whom we feel dependent, whom we fear and whom we love, is nothing but a gigantic projection of the father-image of our youth. In a healthy mind this image dissolves naturally, and the "ego," the feeling of self-reliance, takes its place. But due to all kinds of circumstances this father-image in some people does not disappear, but it is projected and becomes a god. This projection is, of course, harmful for the development of one's personality, and people will never become sound and mature men and women as long as they live under the spell of this self-made god.

That is something of what certain philosophers and anthropologists have suggested regarding the origin and essence of religion. They assumed that religion is a human quality, that it belongs to our human structure, and up to that point they were still unanimous. But they parted company when it came to the evaluation of this phenomenon. Some were inclined to place religion among the beneficial gifts of nature, while others believed that this is true only as far as primitive man is concerned. He needs religion; it is the atmosphere in which he lives; but modern man is mature enough to dispense with it. He can take the reins of his life in his own hands. Finally, there were some who could see religion only as something obnoxious, as a quality of the unhealthy man.

But there is a second possibility. It is possible to believe that religion by its very nature is a response. It is not just a human characteristic, properly part of our equipment. In his religion man feels that he is addressed by a supernatural power, that a god reveals and manifests himself to him. Religion is the human answer to divine, or at least allegedly divine, revelation. This response includes a variety of acts and attitudes. It means faith, surrender, prayer; it implies a feeling of guilt and a craving for salvation; it manifests itself in service and obedience. Religion is never a soliloquy, a dialogue of a man with himself. One of the first assumptions of every religion is that there are divine powers which interfere in our existence, and that there are gods or spirits who speak to us and deal with us. It is true that these gods sometimes seem to be the products of our own imagination, but even then it is clear that religion can only exist in the form of a response. In his religion man is aware that he is not alone, because he knows that he is living in the immediate presence of someone who is infinitely greater than he is.

Is this awareness a lie, or perhaps just imagination? Here we reach a territory where we are beyond the boundaries of what human reason can prove or disprove. A Christian is quite sure that there is divine revelation, that God really speaks to man and concerns Himself with man. He acknowledges that this view is not based upon reasoning, but is instead a matter of faith. In Jesus Christ, God reveals Himself to man and wrestles with man. There is only one adequate answer to this self-revelation of God — and that is humble surrender and a faithful reception of God's merciful love which has appeared to us in Jesus Christ. God's self-disclosure in Jesus Christ is the root of His search for man and His ceaseless speaking to him. From age to age He addressed man and called him to repentance and conversion. The history of mankind is more than just a long account of what man has done, created and invented; its deepest mystery is the story of God's concern with man and man's response to God's revelation. Religion is by its very nature a communion, in which man answers and reacts to God's revelation.

This definition implies that there is a divine revelation, an act of self-disclosure on the part of God. It also implies that there is a human response to this self-disclosure, either in a negative or in a positive sense. Religion can be a profound and sincere seeking of God; it can also be a flight from God, an endeavor to escape from His presence, under the guise of love and obedient service. At the bottom of it lies a relationship, an encounter.

RELIGION AND CULTURE

In this connection it is necessary to say a few words about the relationship between religion and culture. Our starting point is that religion is a human response to what is believed to be a revelation or manifestation of divine powers. It is obvious that we are now speaking of religion as a personal act and relationship. In the history of mankind, however, religion almost always appears to be a social phenomenon. Man acts collectively, especially when he responds to what he considers the deepest realities of life. In his response he is conscious of the fact that he is not an individual but a member of a group. He belongs to a religious community, and because of this he experiences communion with the unseen world. Therefore we can say that, although there is a strictly personal element in religion, the great religions of the world have been and still are great social powers, whose influence can hardly be overestimated.

In almost every religion we find a remarkable oscillation between these two tendencies. Sometimes the emphasis is quite strongly on the system of thought, tradition and practice which belongs to the community as a whole, but every now and then the interest may shift to the personal experiences, the emotions and longings of the individual believer.

In Islam the theological heritage of the first centuries after Mohammed's hegira has played a dominant part. The tenets of the great scholars and the customs of the faithful believers of those days still have an almost unshakable authority. Nevertheless this religion has left room for personal piety during all the centuries of its history. Islamic mysticism is characterized by its own specific approach to the great problems of religious life; and, notwithstanding its emphasis upon the needs and the pilgrimage of the individual believer, it has always been tolerated.

Hinduism is a strong social force. Its moral regulations as they have come to expression in the caste system have framed the life of the people who practise it. Yet this religion has always left room for lonely travelers to withdraw themselves from the community and to pursue the object of becoming one with the immense glory of God in solitary hermitage. In Christianity, traditions and customs have always been an influential force. The individual believer knew that he was a member of the Church and that its creeds and ethical standards dominated his life. Yet the history of the Church shows that frequently people who individually sought God ventured to resist the authority of the leading men in the Church and like trailblazers tried to find new ways of communion with Christ for the sake of finding God.

This short survey shows that religion necessarily has a dual

aspect. It is a personal response to what is considered supernatural revelation; it is a personal decision, a personal surrender, a secret between the individual and his God. On the
other hand, there is no other realm of human life where the
individual is so much a part of the community to which he
belongs as the religious life. Facing the inscrutable mysteries
of the unseen world, man realizes that he is a member of a
community, and that his actions and reactions are an aspect
of the life of that community.

The undeniable fact that religion has a social character
automatically implies that it has considerable influence upon
the development of the group's culture. Bronislaw Malinowsky
has rightly pointed out that it is not "a cultural epiphenomenon
but a profound moral and social force which gives the ultimate
integration to human culture." That is why every aspect of
culture originates from religious sources. Music and dance,
science and medicine, agriculture and architecture have religious roots and originally had a religious character. Hence
it is not correct to say that culture is nothing but a system of
customs and traditions inherited from the forefathers, for it is
more than that. Culture, in so far as it is real culture and not
just an agglomerate of various elements which are not wholly
integrated and not adjusted to each other, is based upon the
fundamental attitude of man toward the universe and the invisible powers. This position implies his social relationships
as well as his attitude towards nature, his sense of responsibility, his outlook upon life and death and his whole system
of evaluations. All these various cultural elements are nothing
but symptoms of the deeper existential attitude of man in the
amazing complexity of the world in which he finds himself.
And it is beyond doubt that this existential attitude bears a
religious character from the very beginning.

One of the striking aspects of modern civilization seems to

---

1 Bronislaw Malinowsky, *The Dynamics of Culture Change*. New Ha-
ven: Yale University Press, 1945, p. 48.

be that it has gradually loosened the ties with its religious background. This is what we usually call the process of secularization by which our modern world is affected. There is much in this process for which we have every reason to be very thankful. We are much freer and more self-conscious than our ancestors were. We know that the ordinary things of life are only things, which we can take up and do with what we want to. There are no taboos retarding our progress; there is no superstitious anxiety hampering our development. Our science and art, our agriculture and our medical science, have created a freedom and a maturity which previous generations did not even dream of. But, on the other hand, we begin to understand that this whole process evokes a disintegration of life which in the long run may prove to be disastrous. There are disconcerting aspects of our civilization which are threatening to suffocate us. The main cause of our predicament obviously lies in the fact that we have neglected the basic problems of culture. We have forgotten that our culture, too, is rooted in a specific existential attitude, and that this attitude is by virtue of its essence a religious phenomenon. Sometimes it looks to me as if our modern civilization is speeding on without knowing where it is going or whither it is drifting, and as though it had lost sight of the ultimate realities with which every human enterprise is confronted. But all the while our modern civilization is undergoing its trial. It is spreading all over the world and fascinating peoples of remote countries, not seldom intoxicating them and filling their hearts with a burning desire to acquire the same freedom, power, and prosperity. But at the same time it is creating a strange vacuum in their lives, and it has an impoverishing effect on their social and religious feelings. It is time for us to acknowledge frankly that our modern civilization, disintegrated though it may seem, is based upon certain presuppositions about man, his place in the world and his responsibility towards God, and that this implies a definite world view, an outlook upon the function of the individual in the community and upon the greatness and the misery of man. We owe this to the peoples to whom we are bringing the products of our scientific endeavors and with whom we are engaged in discussions. The history of the world compels us to reflect upon the course which we have taken in the development of our civilization and as soon as we begin to do so we shall see that modern culture, too, is a religious phenomenon, either in the positive or in the negative sense.

CHAPTER II

RELIGIONS AND RELIGIOUS
CONSCIOUSNESS

However far we look into the history of mankind, in every period we find religion to be one of the most striking aspects of human life. As far back as the old civilizations of Mesopotamia, Egypt, China and other parts of the world, religion played an important role. It seems that it has always accompanied man on the long way of his gradual development and has never left him. Speaking of our modern world, the well-known English poet T. S. Eliot says:

> But it seems that something has happened that has never happened before: though we know not just when, or why, or how, or where. Men have left God not for other gods, they say, but for no god; and this has never happened before.[1]

Indeed, "this has never happened before," for it is not quite certain even of modern man whether he is as much deprived of religious feeling as he pretends to be. Perhaps we had better not speak of religion in the singular but in the plural, for we are confronted with an amazing variety of religions when we

---

[1] T. S. Eliot, "Choruses from *The Rock*," Chorus VII.

trace the history of civilization. We meet religions which impress us with their almost unbelievable cruelty, involving head-hunting, the sacrifice of children, the burning of widows on their husbands' funeral pyres, the extirpation of all those who ventured to act in defiance of the old traditions. An immense quantity of blood has been shed for the sake of religion. But, on the other hand, religion has also been the source of very noble and creative deeds. It has made saints and heroes of men, it has taught man to love his neighbor and to deny himself. Indeed, it is better not to generalize, but rather to make an effort to specify and classify the various religious trends.

It is no wonder that many endeavors have already been made in this direction since the science of comparative religion started its research. At first it seems quite obvious to make a sharp distinction between primitive and more rational and civilized religions. In primitive religions nature itself is regarded, and treated, as a divine being; but in civilized religions man understands that God is a spiritual power, highly exalted above this phenomenal world. When the German philosopher Hegel tried to classify the various religions, he spoke of nature religions or primitive religions, then of religions in which God is seen as a spiritual personality, and finally of the perfect religion in which the finite and the infinite are united.

Although this division between primitive and more rational religions is quite understandable, it involves serious difficulties. Our main objection is that it borrows its standards of division not from religion itself but from sophisticated intellectual systems. This mistake had already been made by some of the Apostolic Fathers and Apologists of the first centuries. They were inclined to despise the mythical religion of ancient Greece, as described by Homer and Hesiod, and took for granted that the more rationalistic religion of Heraclitus and Socrates was much closer to the Christian message. In their opinion the *logos,* or reason, of which Greek philosophy speaks was the same *Logos* spoken of in the Gospel of John. Obviously they did not understand clearly enough that although the whole approach of Greek philosophy was different from that of the older myths, there was nevertheless closer affinity between these philosophical systems and the so-called mythical religion of previous centuries than they had assumed. Although this distinction is somewhat justified, it nevertheless does not take us very far. Both primitive and rationalistic religion, though different in their ways of expressing themselves, may be almost identical in their outlook upon the fundamental relationships which are so essential in every religion.

Ernst Troeltsch, in his classification of religions, approached the problem from a different angle.[2] He divided the various religions in two groups, soteriological and legalistic religions. There are religions which emphasize so strongly that man must obey certain laws and regulations that they deserve the name of legalistic religions. Islam can be called a legalistic religion, in so far as it stresses the law of Allah, which every believer must observe wholeheartedly. On the other hand, there are religions which emphasize that we must seek salvation, and that this salvation really exists and can be obtained. Troeltsch was convinced that Christianity as well as the religions of India belong to the soteriological religions, although their conceptions of what salvation is differ greatly.

It seems to me that this distinction is too artificial in some respects. In religious practice, law is not always the opposite of salvation. On the contrary, in various religions the divine law is seen and also experienced as a token of salvation, or at least as an element in the process of salvation. A life really saved is a life in which the law is humbly accepted, and kept with thankfulness. That is why we have to be careful not to overemphasize an aspect which has only a relative value. In his valuable study *Is Christianity Unique?* Nicol Macnicol makes a distinction between those religions which view God as immanent in the world and those which view Him as transcen-

---

2 Ernst Troeltsch, *Die Absolutheit des Christentums und die Religionsgeschichte.* Tübingen: Mohr, 1912, p. 83.

dent over the world. This difference in concept implies a very profound difference in the relationship towards God. Macnicol believes that "both these extremes must be avoided and the middle road discovered." In this connection he quotes in a favorable sense Dr. John Oman, who defended the idea that "there are two types of religious development, one which views the natural as the veiling of the supernatural, the other which views it as revealing."[3] This distinction has some value. It cannot be denied that the problem of the immanence and the transcendence of God is a very crucial matter in the history of religion, but it is doubtful whether this specific point can be used as a principle for division.

A very positive division has been made by Hendrik Kraemer. He thinks that we should distinguish between "prophetic religions of revelation and naturalist religions of transempirical realization. To the first group belong Christianity, Judaism, and, because it is historically and by its nature related to the Christian and Jewish religions, to a certain degree also Islam."[4]

Before Kraemer, other scholars, such as Nathan Soederblom and, following in his footsteps, Friedrich Heiler, had pointed in the same direction. The latter came to the conclusion, through his broad and thorough study on the place of prayer in the various religions, that there are two types of religious piety, the mystical and the prophetic. In mysticism God is not a living and active Will but an eternal and quiescent Majesty; in prophetic religion He is experienced and acknowledged as a living and active power.[5] Is this division practicable; and can it easily be applied? Of course, it is not difficult to raise various objections. Kraemer himself concedes that even the natural religions of transempirical realization are "not entirely ig-

---

[3] Nicol Macnicol, *Is Christianity Unique? A Comparative Study of the Religions.* London: SCM Press, 1936, p. 28.

[4] Hendrik Kraemer, *The Christian Message in a Non-Christian World.* London: The Edinburgh House Press, 1938, p. 142.

[5] Friedrich Heiler, *Das Gebet. Eine Religionsgeschichtiche und Religionspsychologische Untersuchung.* Munich: Reinhardt, 1921, pp. 248-283.

norant of revelation. In a more external sense all religions, not excepting the primitive ones, can be called religions of revelation, because all religions rely on some sort of sacred book or sacred text that is more or less distinctly considered a revelation." Nevertheless, he maintains his own division, and makes the remark that in these natural religions "the center of gravity does not lie in the fact or notion of revelation; it is a subsidiary notion, introduced because revelation is such an essentially religious concept that no religion whatever can do without it."[6] This may be true, but at the same time it is clear that the separation between the two groups is not very sharp. There are sometimes "prophetic" elements in naturalist religions, just as there are "naturalistic" elements in prophetic religions.

Our second objection is that it is doubtful whether the Christian religion can be said to be a "prophetic" religion along with Judaism and Islam. When applied to Christianity the word "prophetic" gets a new and entirely different meaning. For a Christian, Christ is not only, and perhaps not in the first place, a prophet, but He is much more than that. By describing Judaism, Christianity, and Islam as "prophetic" religions, we are compelled to overlook many aspects which cannot be ignored.

The conclusion of our short survey is that, although we may classify the various religions, we are inevitably confronted by serious obstacles. Every classification is to a certain extent justifiable, but it runs the risk of becoming a distortion, or at least an overemphasis, of aspects which are not as central as they seem to be. For that reason I prefer not to make a classification. Instead of dividing the various religions into groups, I proceed from what may be called the "universal religious consciousness." Kraemer mentions this and defines its character: "As both scientific research and critical thinking teach, there is no 'natural' religion: there is only a universal religious consciousness in man, which produces many similarities."[7] It is

---

6 Kraemer, *op. cit.*, pp. 142, 143.
7 *Ibid.*, p. 112.

worth our while to examine this "religious consciousness" and to try to find out why and in which sense it produces so many similarities.

RELIGIOUS CONSCIOUSNESS

This universal religious consciousness is something mysterious. It is not something concrete, something we can grasp and lay hold of. It does not show itself, and we never meet it in its original form. It is vague and nebulous, and we can find it only indirectly, by scrutinizing the various religions in which it has taken shape. It is beyond doubt that antagonistic forces play a part in it. Not infrequently man seems to flee from the same gods whose communion he seeks and whose blessing he craves. Therefore it is not possible to describe this religious consciousness in one word. If we can make any statement about its qualities at all, it is that it is a complicated thing, full of tensions and contrasts.

On the other hand, it strikes us that this consciousness, notwithstanding the fact that it displays so many varieties, has nevertheless a certain continuity. This continuity is only comprehensible when we take into account that men, in spite of the innumerable differences between the various races and peoples, were forced to follow similar trails. Of course, they did so in various ways, every group putting its specific stamp on its religious expressions. But when we survey the religious ideas and customs of all races and peoples, we are impressed by the many resemblances. It has frequently been pointed out that the remarkable phenomenon which is usually called "primitive religion," no matter where it is found, is characterized by certain peculiar features. The myths of the Indian tribes in America are comparable to those of the Bantu tribes in Africa, of the people in remote parts of Asia and the islands of the Pacific. And not only are their myths similar, but their religious rites and customs are also in many respects the same. Still this similarity, astonishing though it may be, is not as strange as some people think. On the contrary, it is rather easy to trace its origin.

In the first place, we must realize the immense importance of the unity of mankind. The human race, now cut into pieces, is a jig-saw puzzle of dissected parts, but there is sufficient reason to believe in its fundamental unity. It is not only possible but even likely that there are still some common traditions which go back to a past that we have no knowledge of. Besides, during the long course of human history there must have been contact between the various peoples, although we are no longer able to see how and when it took place.

In the second place, man is a limited being — limited in every respect. This means that at every crossroad he has only a few choices, and it is incredible on how few ideas mankind has lived. Man is always restricted by his anthropological structure, and, although this structure gives him the chance to make choices among a few possibilities, he cannot outgrow his own qualities and dispositions. That must be the reason why man always returns to the same conceptions and in a monotonous way grasps at the same suppositions again and again.

In the third place, we should not forget that man, by virtue of his place in the world, must always and everywhere give answers to the same questions. He has to struggle with the basic problems which his existence itself entails. He is afflicted by grief and misfortune; he meets both adverse and prosperous conditions; deep in his heart he has a vague feeling of responsibility; he has to adapt himself to the course of nature; he is aware that he is only a very small being in the immeasurable greatness of the universe; and he knows very well that sooner or later death will knock at his door. Wherever he goes, he is surrounded by a multitude of questions, and, although he has the power to escape from them for a certain time, he cannot help being overwhelmed by them at times. His being on earth is itself such an immense riddle that it threatens to crush him. The answers to all the questions with which he has to struggle may be different, but the problems themselves are always the same. And he has to respond to them, not only in his thinking and feeling but also in his whole attitude to life, in his acts and rites, in his existence itself; his whole way of life is a response. Therefore it stands to reason that this universal religious consciousness, with all its antagonisms and tensions, is something real and is to be found wherever men live and toil.

THE FIVE MAGNETIC POINTS

These considerations take us logically to the question: Is it possible to formulate the main points which have drawn the attention of man? Let us call them "magnetic points," because they are points which demand our attention and which we cannot evade. We cannot help being confronted with them. Since they are rooted in our existence, they are stronger than ourselves, and somehow we must come to grips with them. We can define five such magnetic points, or focal points. It is our intention to deal with each of them more elaborately later on, but here we shall confine ourselves to mentioning their names.

The first focus point could be called the sense of cosmic relationship. It means that man feels a relationship with the cosmos. He is but a particle, an atom in the whole of the universe, but he knows that he is akin to the world in which he lives and to which he belongs, and that his life is in intimate relationship with the life of nature. He senses that there is no distance between himself and his environment. The first question man has to face is that of his relation to the cosmos. It can be summarized briefly as the relationship of *I and the cosmos.*

The second point is *the religious norm* with which man is confronted. There is something in his inmost being that warns him not to follow his own desires. He has a vague sense that there are certain rules which he must obey. It is the relationship of *I and the norm.*

In the third place, man comes face to face with the riddle of his existence. He is conscious that he is an active being — he does things; he is always busy. But on the other hand, he is sometimes overtaken by the strange idea that he is the victim of that indefinable something which he is inclined to call his fate or destiny. He stands between these two, *between action and destiny,* and he does not know his exact place. It is the relationship of *I and the riddle of my existence.*

The fourth point is man's *craving for salvation.* There seems to be something in man that compels him to believe that the reality with which he has to do every day is not as it should be. There is something wrong with the world; there are deficiencies that hamper him in his life. It is very hard to say what these deficiencies are, but it is quite certain that they exist. Nature is not as it should be; it is full of disastrous powers, floods and volcanic eruptions, earthquakes and tempests. And not only nature, but also man himself, is not as he ought to be. There is also something wrong in his own existence. That is why we hear that dark and heartbreaking groaning for salvation through all the ages of man's history. Man has that remarkable tendency not to accept reality as it presents itself to him, but he always dreams of a better world in which life will be healthy and safe. It is the relationship of *I and salvation.*

And finally there is the fifth point, that of the reality behind reality. The Greek word for truth (*aletheia*) indicates clearly that there is a certain veil that conceals the deepest grounds of reality. That veil must be removed, the fundamental truth must be revealed. We are living in an imaginary world of which we do not see the substance. Behind the curtain of this phenomenal world there must be an invisible counterpart, a world of spiritual beings — demons or gods or whatever they may be. This strange belief is also very fundamental to man's religious intuitions. Even when he is inclined to break with this belief and to become an atheist in the full sense of the word, he is often still overwhelmed by it, as it were. The idea that there is a *Supreme Power* to which he himself is related is apparently something that he can never get rid of. It is the relationship of *I and the Supreme Power.*

These are the five magnetic questions to which man is inevitably drawn. We cannot speak of them as innate ideas, because they are not a sort of natural religion. They are just questions with which man is confronted through the mere fact that he exists and that he finds himself in a world full of riddles and mysteries. These five questions keep him busy whether he likes it or not.

The answer which he gives to these questions determines his entire conduct and his attitude to life. Even when he never takes the time and the trouble deliberately to ponder on them and to penetrate into them, still his whole way of living already implies an answer, and *is* an answer. That is why we find these five focus points in every religion and in every human life, even in that of the so-called nonreligious man.

PART I

THE CONTINENT OF THE UNIVERSAL
RELIGIOUS CONSCIOUSNESS

CHAPTER III

MAN'S SENSE OF COSMIC RELATIONSHIP

Before we begin our investigations, it is necessary to consider first what the expression "sense of cosmic relationship" implies. It is obvious, to begin with, that man is a unit or particle in the immense whole of the cosmos; he is an atom in the universe.

This elementary fact does not mean, however, that he is always aware of his being a cosmic particle. Man has the remarkable power to create a certain distance between himself and the cosmos, and to place himself upon a platform from which he looks upon the world as if it were something else. Of course, when he falls from a high rock, or is almost starved to death, or is seriously ill, he is reminded in a rather harsh way of his being only a particle; but as soon as he has regained his strength and his safety, he ascends his throne again and wields the scepter over his world. The world becomes his minion again, the object with which he can play his game.

This makes it clear that his sense of cosmic relationship is a specific phenomenon. It means that man does not always place himself upon a platform, and does not always create a distance between himself and the cosmos, but is constantly aware of being part of that cosmos. He belongs to the great cosmic relationship; he feels a certain affinity with the cosmos; everything in the world around him is akin to himself, is as it were a brother or sister to him. The ground which he tills, the rice and the corn which he is allowed to eat, the trees and the flowers, the mountains and the sea, the birds and the animals, they all belong to the same community of which he is a member. They are not just neutral things he handles, but they are cells of the same great body, atoms of the same universe to which he belongs. The rules which are inherent in the world are the same as those which man has to observe in his own existence. Man feels that he can live and breathe only when he is intimately related to nature and is in time with the cosmic rhythm.

When we study the various religions, it immediately strikes us that this sense of cosmic relationship has played an important part in each. Every religion necessarily deals with the place of man in the totality of the universe. Religious man can never see himself as an isolated creature; he knows and experiences all the time that he is integrated into a complex whole and that his life is permanently encompassed by it. That is why it is quite natural that many religions have painstakingly attempted to define this mysterious affinity of man with the cosmos, and have tried to formulate the laws of life which originate from this unity. They have intuitively felt that our well-being is somehow dependent on the way in which we understand and humbly obey the rules of the universe.

PRIMITIVE RELIGION

The first religion we meet on our journey through history is the so-called *primitive religion*. This "primitive religion" is a peculiar and very interesting phenomenon. For a very long time it was looked down upon as something inferior, a ridiculous superstition. During the last century, however, it began to arouse the interest of quite a few missionaries and scholars, some of whom advanced the idea that primitive religion is the primeval form of all religion and that all other religions developed from this "mother-religion." That is why they were eager to study its motives and to find out how the so-called "primitive man" looked at the world. They wanted to know where the gods originated and also how these primitive cultures had come to believe in demons and spirits.

One of the first scholars to feel that primitive religion was not just a ridiculous superstition but deserved our serious attention was Edward Tylor. In 1871 he published his book, *Primitive Culture: Researches into the Development of Mythology, Philosophy, Religion, Language, Art and Custom.* In it he developed the animistic theory of the origin of religion. He made the statement that myth is rooted "in the belief in the animation of all nature," a belief which "at its highest pitch leads to personification."[1] Tylor assumed that the "ancient savage philosophers" had been impressed by two groups of biological questions: "In the first place, what makes the difference between a living body and a dead one; what causes waking, sleep, trance, disease, death? In the second place, what are those human shapes which appear in dreams and visions?"[2] Reasoning thus, primitive man evidently came to the conclusion that there is a "soul" in man, a soul which leaves the body at the moment of death, and can appear to other people in their dreams and visions. Because primitive men usually do not make a sharp distinction between man and beast, they automatically concluded that animals, and even the rice in the fields, were animated. That is why the world in which primitive man exists is entirely different from the world in which we live. In their world, ghosts of the forefathers, and other spirits, live and show their power. It is quite understandable that in primitive religion some of these spirits have gradually received the rank of powerful deities.

---

[1] Edward B. Tylor, *Primitive Culture,* 5th ed. London: John Murray, 1913, p. 285.
[2] *Ibid.,* p. 428.

This animistic theory about the origin of religion was heartily welcomed by many students of comparative religion. It seemed to offer a rather simple and acceptable solution to the very difficult problem of the origin of religion. Shortly after the appearance of Tylor's book it became clear, however, that primitive religion is a much more complicated phenomenon than he had assumed. Closer research and more accurate consideration resulted more and more in the conviction that some of these so-called primitive religions display an all-including world view and a remarkable unity of outlook, and that the fear of the dead is only an element in them.

At the same time it became evident that primitive religion, inferior though it may seem, is characterized by a surprising tenacity. It is not easy to extirpate, and when it is destroyed, under the pressure of many factors, it leaves a vacuum and retains the power to revive. Moreover, it has the capacity to penetrate, covertly or overtly, other religions, while maintaining its own character within these. It is a matter of fact that many elements of primitive religion have been integrated in Islam as well as in the Indian religions, as they are practiced by the majority of their adherents. And it is well known that in certain Christian churches the influence of primitive religion has been visible for many centuries and is still traceable in our own day.

Other striking features of primitive religion are its widespread diffusion and its remarkable uniformity. We find primitive religion in almost every part of the world, either as a remnant of bygone days or as a still-living and powerful religion. And wherever we find it, we are surprised by its undeniable congruity. That does not, however, mean that there is only one type of primitive religion, and that there are not innumerable variations in the regions where it is found. Not only the tribal organization, but also the religious customs and rites, often have a local or regional character which varies everywhere. Climate and the natural environment, the quality of the soil, and many other factors have made an impact upon the development of primitive religion and given it its specific nature. But notwithstanding this diversity, it remains a fact that there exists an astonishing resemblance between the myths and rites of the primitive people in the most remote parts of the world. This resemblance has led to the idea that in primitive religion we meet a kind of mentality that is different from that of modern man. The French scholar Levy-Bruhl, in an effort to describe its characteristics, has said that primitive man's way of perceiving things and of reasoning — at least when he is acting collectively — differs greatly from our logic. Although he has definitely brought very interesting details of primitive life to light, we now feel that he frequently exaggerates the difference between so-called primitive and modern mentality.

The point that interests us is the question of how primitive religion explains the place of man in the totality of the universe. Let us give an example. In the southeastern part of the island of Borneo live a people called the Ngaju Dayak. A Swiss missionary who has worked among them for many years has given us an elaborate description of the ancient myths and the ritual of this tribe.[3] In his book he tells us that, according to the myths of the Ngaju Dayak, there is a supreme deity which appears as the god of heaven and at the same time as the goddess of the earth. The heavenly god is worshipped under the name of Mahatala, while the goddess of the earth is called Jata. Mahatala is depicted as a gigantic bird, the bird of heaven; Jata is described as a water serpent. This twofold deity existed from the beginning, and the first creature born from this divine being was the glorious tree of life. It is interesting to note that this tree of life plays a predominant part in the myths of nearly all primitive people. Usually it is regarded as the primeval unity, the spring of life, and the origin of nature with all its various aspects.

The Ngaju Dayak myth goes on to mention the destruction

[3] H. Schärer, *Die Gottesidee der Ngadju Dajak in Süd-Borneo.* Leiden: Brill, 1946.

of this tree of life. Both Mahatala and Jata took part in this destructive act. The branches and twigs, the leaves and roots were tossed around, till the whole tree was broken up into a multitude of particles. Apparently this primeval sacrifice is the origin of the immense variety of animals, plants and things with which we are surrounded. In his study on *The Myth of the Eternal Return* Mircea Eliade points out that in "certain archaic cosmogonies the world was given existence through the Sacrifice of a primordial monster, symbolizing chaos (Tiamat), or through that of a cosmic giant (Ymir, Pan-Ku, Purusha)."[4] That is true. We may add that in some myths it is the sacrifice of the tree of life that constitutes the world.

According to the Ngaju Dayak, the world still displays the traces of its twofold origin. We still see the sky and the earth, the immense light of heaven and the dark and mysterious ground upon which we live. Actually we exist between these two; we are, as it were, surrounded by the god we originated from. That is why the tribe, too, consists of two parts. One part is closely related to Mahatala and represents him in the earthly sphere, while the other part is intimately connected with Jata. A natural conclusion is that a son of the heavenly part must marry a daughter of the earthly part. Only thus the structure and the well-being of the universe can be upheld. This remarkable conception shows that in the world view of these people, theology, cosmology and sociology are interrelated and interdependent. The architectural pattern of the cosmos is a reflection of the two aspects of the god of creation, while the social pattern of the tribe is a reflection of the world.

Two more points deserve our attention. The first is that the Ngaju Dayak like to represent a house as an image of the world. A house is much more than merely a place where men live together; in its deepest sense it is a micro-organism in which everything has its well-ordered place. Although this is

---

[4] Mircea Eliade, *The Myth of the Eternal Return.* Tr. by Willard R. Trask. N. Y.: Pantheon Books, 1954 (Bollingen Series Number XLVI), p. 20.

true of every house, it is especially noticeable in a sacral house and in their drawings of houses buried with their dead. These drawings clearly show that the house rests on a vaulted hill, which resembles an ocean wave, because the water serpent, Jata, goddess of the earth, is its basis. The roof of the house resembles a mountain, on top of which there is an umbrella, the general symbol of the tree of life. Obviously the roof represents Mahatala, the god of the heavenly region. Hence the drawing is a kind of "catechism" in a nutshell — it explains in a few lines and symbols the structure of the sacred world.

In some respects the simplicity of these pictures is apt to astonish us. On the other hand we should remember that there are elements in it which are to be found almost everywhere. Several writers have pointed out that sacral buildings, temples and other holy houses are usually built in the form of a microcosm. This was already done in the ancient world, in Babylon and Egypt, and it is still done in India and other countries of the Far East. It seems as if man has understood from the very beginning that a house is a sacred place, and that it can only be called a house in the full sense of the word when its architecture is a depiction of the structure of the cosmos, the house of the gods. Almost everywhere among the Ngaju Dayak we find a pond near the temple, a representation of the primeval ocean, while the roof or the towers represent the mountain of the gods. There is nearly always a tree of life or a cosmic tree, and every temple has a center, an extremely holy part, where the visible world is believed to come in touch with the invisible.[5]

The second point to be mentioned is that in the life of the Ngaju Dayak, religious rites are regarded as a repetition or a representation of the cosmogonic acts. As the destruction of the tree of life resulted in the richness and variety of our present world, so religious rites are supposed to produce prosperity and happiness. When the tribe is going through a time

---

[5] Robert Heine-Geldern, *Weltbild und Bauform in Süd-Ostasien* (Weiner Beiträge zur Kunst und Kulturgeschichte Asiens). Vienna: 1930.

of hardship and sorrow, a tree of life is planted in the center
of the village; afterwards this tree is destroyed with the express
purpose of creating a renewal of safety and life. As Eliade
says, "Man is contemporary with the cosmogony and with the
anthropogony because ritual projects him into the mythical
epoch of the beginning."[6] This applies not only to the religion
of the Ngaju Dayak, but also to many other religions. Generally speaking, we may say that religious rites usually are intended
to transport those who participate in them back to the time
before times, the mysterious "in the beginning." "The beginning" is the source of life and the return to it, even in a merely
symbolical way, involves the inauguration of a new epoch.

The religion of the Ngaju Dayak is an amazingly elaborate
example of what we can call a primitive apprehension of reality.
On the other hand, its whole outlook is simple and easy to
grasp. There are other religions which give us a much more
complicated picture of the world and of human life. In these
we meet not just a bipolar universe with a heavenly god and
an earthly goddess, but four or five different parts, answering to
the points of the compass, the center included. Each has a
specific character and is related to different phenomena. The
east is obviously connected with the birth of light, with the
color red, with the king and the palace, and with many other
glorious things. The south is the region of life in its maturity
and fullness. The west, on the contrary, is related to death
and darkness and, since it is taken for granted that the way
to everlasting knowledge passes through death, the west is
also the region of truth and science. The north is often viewed
as the place of death. Hence the village cemetery is to be found
at the northern end. Each of the four parts has its own color,
is characterized by specific flowers and trees, and is related
to specific stars and celestial phenomena. It is indeed a "classi-
fied" world in which these peoples live. Therefore the palace
of the king and the temple — if there is such a building —

---

[6] Eliade, *op. cit.,* p. 22.

always face east. The trees and flowers which are found in the garden of the chief are not planted at random, because everything has its own value and place in the whole of the cosmos. A bride is decked with specific flowers which in a symbolical form show the secrets of marriage; plants revealing the mystery of death grow in the graveyard. Nothing in nature is absolutely neutral; everything has its own place and its own significance. The witch doctor, who knows all about these things, can show the people how everything must be organized and which days or hours are suitable for certain activities.

There is, of course, much more to be said of primitive religion, but what we have seen thus far makes it sufficiently clear that primitive man's self-consciousness is different from ours. In primitive religion self-consciousness necessarily implies man's consciousness of the place he occupies in the cosmic world. Men are tiny particles in the mysterious cosmos; they belong to it, try to reflect on it and to live in time with its rhythm. The cosmos is not their object; it is not something that they must conquer and place in subjection. Rather, it is their origin; they are part of it. The meaning of primitive man's life is that he is a microcosmos, in which the various aspects of the cosmos are reflected. The cosmos is an overwhelming great and sacred community, and men are members of it. Therefore their whole conduct is determined by the laws and rules of the cosmos as a whole.

HINDUISM

When we turn to Hinduism, it immediately strikes us that similar phenomena can be observed there. Hinduism is a very remarkable system of thoughts and practices. Speaking of it, Nehru says: "Hinduism as a faith is vague, amorphous, many-sided, all things to all men."[7] And yet this religion proves to be a fascinating power, and a storehouse of profound ideas

[7] Jawaharlal Nehru, *The Discovery of India*. Calcutta: The Signet Press, 1946, p. 53.

GOSHEN COLLEGE LIBRARY
GOSHEN, INDIANA

about man and his place in the universe. Already many centuries ago the great philosophers of India meditated on the origin of this remarkable world. The conclusions to which they came, which they handed down to their disciples, are formulated in the Vedas, the sacred books of Hinduism. It is in one of these, the so-called Rig-Veda, that the birth of the world is described as follows: In the beginning there was nothing but the primeval ocean, that immense and unformed being, which is called Tad Ekam, "That One." For some mysterious reason Prajapati, "the Lord of creatures," entered into this Tad Ekam as an *hiranya garbha,* a golden seed. As soon as the seed had permeated the ocean, the ocean began to be creative. The potentialities which were hidden in it began to manifest themselves, and that is how this world with all its different and frequently antagonistic forces has come into being. As we have already observed in primitive religion, the idea that people cherish concerning the origin of the world has a dominating influence upon their religious attitude and rites. No wonder also that in India the cosmogonic act is repeatedly represented in ritual. The ritual contemporizes us with primeval time. For that reason, in the religious rites, the *pujas,* the primeval ocean is represented by a pot or jar, the so-called *kalsa* or *kumba.* This pot is put in the center of the sacrificial place. At the beginning of the ceremony the priest solemnly drops a coin into it, which reminds the people of the golden seed which entered into the ocean in the beginning. Hence that which took place at the creation of the world is re-enacted in the religious rite. It is as if we find ourselves present at the dawn of creation and as if we ourselves are playing a part in it. That is why this pot is invoked before the gods are worshipped. Moreover, the primeval ocean is the origin not only of men but also of the gods. The gods of fire and water, of fertility and destruction are born from Tad Ekam.

The very old idea of Prajapati who penetrated the primeval ocean has been explained in a more sophisticated way in the Upanishads and has influenced Indian thinking during all the centuries of its development. It has also exercised a stimulating influence on Indian art. In many temples we find sculptured reliefs in which a *padma,* a lotus flower with a remarkably thick stalk, is shown. This thick part is called the *padma-mula,* the root of the lotus. Since the lotus itself represents the cosmos in its vastness and variety of aspects, it seems likely that this *padma-mula* represents the golden seed.

The Indian people have been deeply impressed by what they consider the perpetual war between the powers of order and chaos. The gods, the *devas,* are the defenders of harmony and order; the demons are the creators of chaos. In the world the gods are represented by the heroes, while the demons are incarnate in giants. The famous epic poems of Indian literature narrate a multitude of stories in which this war is vividly painted. In actual life the powers of chaos manifest themselves in storms and earthquakes, in seasons of-extreme drought and floods. But the gods are always ready and able to resist their archenemies and to defeat them. This does not mean, however, that there will come a period when the demonic forces will be completely annihilated, for this is not so. They have a legitimate place in the cosmos, since they, too, originate from the mysterious Tad Ekam. It is true that they are defeated time and again, but they will never be extirpated. Hence there is not a very clear distinction between the gods and the demons. Some of the gods seem to possess the characteristics of both; they are creators of wealth and prosperity and at the same time demolishing powers. At times they destroy the world which they built. It is especially Shiva, sculptured as Nataraja, the Divine Dancer, who shows in a certain statue that he brings forth worlds according to his pleasure, but that he likewise does not hesitate to annihilate them by the fire of his destructive force. The Indian people believe that man is living in a mysterious world of riddles which are utterly inscrutable. Man does not know what he is and cannot fathom the depths of the mystery of his existence, but the more man reflects on the reality of life, the more he is persuaded that the same contrasting powers of order and chaos are also present in his own heart. In that sense he himself appears to be a microcosmos, a tiny mirror of the complexity of the universe.

One of the most intriguing features of Indian religion is that it has built its doctrine of salvation on the basis of this conception. Although it is hardly possible to speak of the Indian doctrine of salvation in the singular, we can make an endeavor to give a general survey of the main aspects of it.

The first aspect is that it is rather pessimistic. Its tenet is that this strange, ambivalent world is, by virtue of its origin, nothing but vanity and failure. There is no lasting happiness in it, and man will never succeed in achieving a state of real bliss. The very fact that we are human beings implies that we are subjected to *samsara,* transiency of existence, and that we are living in the bondage of ignorance. Therefore there is only one feasible way of escape left to every man who is aware of his wretchedness. Such a man must turn his back upon the magic spell of the world and seek his salvation in solitary meditation. By passing through the stages of this serious meditation he will gradually discover the primeval light out of which everything is born. His eye will be turned away from the embarrassing multitude of phenomena with which he is confronted, and he will return to the spring and origin of everything, the Tad Ekam of the beginning, the mysterious glory of Brahman. This Brahman, in his state of not-being-evolved (*a-vyaktam*), will fascinate him more and more and free him from the temptations of ordinary life. Along this painful path the solitary pilgrim will regain his oneness with Brahman; he will be absorbed in the greatness of that which was in the beginning. That means that the genesis of the world has to be undone, every step of it has to be retraced, till the final goal is reached and self-consciousness is completely lost in the great vision of Brahman. This trend of thinking has moved thousands of religious heroes to say farewell to this transitory world. Its tenets are posited in the Upanishads and elaborated in the Vedantic systems of philosophy and religion.

Besides this rather pessimistic outlook there is also a more positive attitude. This has found its clearest exposition in the Bhagavad Gita, the famous dialogue between the hero Arjuna and his charioteer, Krishna. Krishna appears to be an *avatara,* an incarnation of the supreme god, from whom this world originated. In this discourse it is by no means denied that the world in which we are living has the character of delusion and can never satisfy our hearts, which crave for everlasting salvation. Nevertheless the divine teacher makes a serious appeal to the sense of responsibility of his royal pupil. He shows him that man is allowed to remain in this world and to fulfill the task his caste requires of him, provided he does it with an attitude of detachment. In doing his duty man has to refrain from becoming too much interested in the results of his work. This principle is called *nish-kama-karma,* that is, to perform one's action (*karma*) without being anxious to reap fruits from it (*kama*). If a man can conquer his passions and perform his task in society without aiming at honor or pleasure or riches, he is perfectly free, and his work will not hamper him in any way. "The world is imprisoned in its own activity, except when actions are performed as worship of God. Therefore you must perform every action sacramentally, and be free from all attachments to results."[8]

When we try to penetrate the deeper backgrounds of Indian religion, it strikes us that in this religion man is seen as a cell in the body of the totality, a part of the great cosmic community. His existence on earth is only a wave in the immense ocean of infinity. Man recognizes himself in the divine and demonic powers which exist everywhere in the universe. He knows that he is related to everything around him. To be a human being means in the deepest sense to be a microcosm, a focus point, where all the powers of the cosmos converge. Man can look at this strange world with all her antagonistic forces and say, "That's me! I am one with you!"

---

8 Bhagavad Gita. N. Y.: Mentor, n.d. (Mentor Religious Classic), p. 45.

The absorbing thing in Indian religion is that at the same time it teaches its adherents that there is something inside man that transcends the confusing abundance of the cosmos. This mysterious quality in man (which has no inner contradictions) is the *tad-ekam.* Just as the great world was born out of the cosmic Tad Ekam (which is not differentiated), so this *tad-ekam* still lies at the bottom of human existence. It is hidden behind man's thoughts and imaginations, his passions and emotions, in the abysmal depth of his existence. He can find it only on the long road of self-denial and struggle against the desires of his own heart. But when this Tad Ekam, this divine power, finally imprisons him and begins to rule over him, he finds rest and complete peace. In one of the philosophic schools of India, the *samkhya,* man's innermost being, is often compared with a spectator, a *sakshin.* He is not active himself, he is never concerned in the great drama of our existence. From the impenetrable depths he sees the game of our life, until we ourselves wake up and rid ourselves of that game because it is not real. Then only man begins to understand fully that this bewildering world, with its continuous pressures and struggles, which has enchanted and fascinated him all during his existence, is only a delusion, and that he, in spite of his deepest involvement, has never really belonged to it.

SURVEY

It is not possible to continue our journey and have a look at all the different religions, nor is it necessary. A bird's-eye view already shows us that there are analogous ideas in nearly all religions.

The ancient religions of Egypt and Babylon have carefully attempted to determine man's place in the totality of the cosmos. Egyptian religion tells of the primeval waters, the *nun* out of which the primeval hillock rose in the beginning. From this hill the different gods originated. Therefore every temple is still a memorial of the primeval hillock from which everything sprung. During his whole life man is in relationship with the cosmic powers that hold him and decide his fate on earth.

In ancient Mesopotamia the cosmos was thought to be large and broad. The constellations, going their mysterious ways in breathless silence through the depths of the universe, belonged to it. They determined our weal and woe; for human life is taken up in the wonderful coherence of heaven and earth.

China has known from time immemorial the contrast between Yang and Yin. Yang is the light and sunlit side of the mountain; it is bright and luminous; it means summer, heaven, masculinity. Yin is the shady side, darkness; it stands for winter, night, earth, femininity. The universe only exists by grace of the balance between these two. At a certain time of the year it seems as if the darkness gets the upper hand and the universe is unbalanced. Then the emperor used to bring his sacrifice to the gods on the big altar so that order would be restored in the universe. Thus man's life balances constantly between these two cosmic powers. A wise man is he who is able to keep the plants in his garden, the food he eats, indeed his whole manner of life well balanced. In China, too, human life is thought to be taken up in the cosmic coherence.

We may ask whether this feeling of belonging to the cosmic unity still exists in our modern world. It can certainly be said that man has learned to subject the world and use it for his own purposes. Let us, for instance, compare the ways in which different peoples of the East cultivate their land with our own modern agricultural methods. These peoples, who do not dare to tamper with the normal cause of nature, use it according to their needs, after having performed certain ceremonies at every step to propitiate the spirits of nature. As a rule a member of these groups will not kill an animal if he has not asked the gods' permission beforehand, and has not said that it is not for himself but to be used as a sacrifice to them. These people have a sense of awe and respect for nature. It is not simply an "it" with which mankind can do as it wills; it is a divine entity to which he himself belongs and of which he is a part.

Modern Western civilization is basically different. Modern man stands as it were on a platform above nature, and he knows that it is subjected to him. He drives his tractors across the land and bores his tunnels through the mountains. This "platform feeling" is very characteristic of modern man. Now that our modern technical civilization begins to penetrate the utmost corners of the world, this entirely different attitude toward nature causes tensions everywhere. The agricultural aid which we give to nations introduces a rapid social change and an altogether new viewpoint with regard to nature. This is one of the great problems of our time.

Has the sense of being a particle in the great cosmic unity altogether vanished in our modern world? Certainly not. It still lives on in art and music, in literature and sculpture. In art man still knows to some degree that he is an atom in the cosmos, a very small cell in the immense body of the universe. But in his daily life it has been pushed to the background; it no longer occupies such a central place as it used to do in times past. Man today still has a vague idea that he does not know just where he stands in the cosmos. He feels lost and confused. He gropes for a new vision with regard to the world and himself. It must be absorbing to examine what the gospel of Jesus Christ has to say on this subject. We shall apply ourselves to this matter later on.

CHAPTER IV

THE RELIGIOUS NORM

The very fact that we are human beings inevitably confronts us with standards of behavior. We need not go into this, for it stands very much to reason. The well-known cultural anthropologist, Bronislaw Malinowsky, speaking of the essence of culture, says that the "normative" aspect may be called a "universal aspect of culture." He sees this aspect as a necessary consequence of people living in communities: "Both co-operation and life in common imply sacrifices and joint effort, subordination of private interest to mutual gain — in short, the existence of rules, authority and of constraint."[1]

An individual man, or a group of people, may forget and break the existing rules for some time; they may make a stand against the existing authority and overthrow it; but they will never succeed in denying all rules and every authority, because to do so would be to destroy every form of society. Hence it seems justifiable to explain the existence of moral norms and a system of moral values as the results of the demands of community life. Every community assumes that the individuals belonging to it cannot let their fancies run away with them, but that they must listen to others and reckon with their interests.

[1] Malinowsky, *The Dynamics of Culture Change,* pp. 44f.

Let us begin at the beginning. A child grows up in a family and comes into contact with other members from his earliest days. In his childhood he must obey his parents and try to find his place in the family or in the circle in which he is brought up. Even in this early period of his life, man encounters rules, authority and constraint. Later on, the horizon of his existence widens; he begins to understand that he belongs to a clan or a tribe or a people, and he comes in touch with the customs and laws that dominate the life of that particular tribe or people. Thus man's confrontation with norms right from the beginning is one of the fundamental aspects of human life.

It is, however, sufficiently clear that the existence of moral rules cannot be exclusively explained by the necessity that man adapt himself to the life of the community, although this is very important. All over the world we see that the norms to which man knew himself to be subjected were felt as a divine institution. Man is apt to consider these norms not just as sensible rules to safeguard community life; he feels that their origin lies deeper and that their authority is therefore greater. He feels that these norms have a divine origin. That is why a certain system of norms is integrated into every living religion. This thought immediately raises a very difficult question, for there is a certain friction between "the sense of cosmic relationship," as we have called it, and the idea of a divine norm. A sense of cosmic relationship implies a conviction of being part of the enormous cosmic family, of being a tiny cell in the great body of the universe. As soon as this conviction begins to dominate our thoughts we can do nothing but move along in the rhythm of the cosmic process. Our own point of view no longer matters, because we are only atoms in a larger entity. We cannot simply go our own way, but from birth till death we are carried along by the cosmic rhythm. We may imagine that we are deciding our own conduct and career, but that is only a childish illusion. We are nothing and can do nothing. Our greatest illusion is implied by the little word "I." When we use this word, we keep aloof from the world, we look upon ourselves as not belonging to the world, and we regard the world as our subject. In short, the sense of cosmic relationship is opposed to this illusion, for it has no room for human personality.

The consciousness of a religious norm, on the other hand, strengthens our self-consciousness. This norm appeals to our will and responsibility. It tells us that we are not merely a speck of dust or an ocean wave, but assumes that we can make our own choices, that we are free. The very fact that we are human is presupposed by this norm. It denies that we can live only in accordance with the cosmic process. It consistently reminds us that we are different from the stars, which can only run their prescribed courses. It tells us that we are different from a tree or a flower which can obey the laws of life. We are even different from the animals. We are responsible — that is to say, we will have to give an account of our actions.

There is, therefore, a certain friction between these two ideas which are both found in the different religions of mankind. Perhaps it can be said that this is one of the predominant problems with which every religion has to struggle. To help solve this problem we shall try to give a resumé of what has been said about norms by these various religions. It stands to reason that we shall often touch upon that strange friction inherent in these norms.

In primitive religion it is generally emphasized that its norms were handed down by the people's ancestors. These ancestors discovered and formulated them, and guard them. Consequently, every offence against morals is seen as a crime against the ancestors, so it is important to try to keep in continual contact with them.

But who are these ancestors? To a tribe they are more than merely human forbears whose way of life resembled that of the tribe. They are surrounded by a kind of nimbus of divineness. They are closer to the prehistoric times when all things were ordered and the rules for human society were made. When heaven and earth were separated, every creature received its

own place in the great totality of the cosmos, and man was also
given a place in it. All this happened in prehistoric times, that
beginning of all times when the meaning and norm of all future
events were conceived. Old myths relate that the ancestors
descended from gods, and that something of the divine wisdom
was in them. When they settled on that plot of earth where the
tribe now lives they drew up rules according to which everything would have to be regulated from then on. They fixed
the division of the tribe, and how the various clans were to behave towards each other. They particularly regulated the laws
of marriage, for, after all, marriage is, or at least is meant to be,
a reflection of the great cosmic marriage of heaven and earth,
of light and dark. The ancestors saw all these things clearly
and passed them on to their children. These ancient rules,
which are mysteriously whispered to the mature boy on the
occasion of his initiation, are holy and inviolable. As long as
the tribe maintains and obeys these rules, all its activities will
be blessed. The ancestors did not actually create the social
and moral regulations — they saw them, discovered them, deduced them from the structure of the cosmos. They were in
closer contact with the mystery of the world and so they knew
things which their descendants cannot know. But the actual
creators of the rules were the gods, who in the beginning caused
this strange world, with all its contrary powers, to be born. The
myths of numerous peoples made mention of the existence of
a High God or Supreme Being in the beginning, who ordered
this world and established its regulations. Little is told about
him, and generally he is not regularly invoked, but it is always emphasized that it was he who created order when there
was only chaos and that he still maintains this order. Some of
these myths mysteriously add that the High God, after ordering
all things, journeyed to a far land, to make it plausible why he
occupies such a small place in the religious life of the tribe
or people. Historians of religion, in speaking of these high
gods, sometimes describe them as *"Garantie der Weltord-*

nung."[2] They say that they were necessary to foster a belief in a higher power responsible for the rules and laws. Since every tribe considers a year as a short summary of the great cosmic year, i.e., the whole period of the world, there is a short period once a year which reminds of and reflects prehistoric times when chaos still reigned and no laws had yet been introduced. This was the time, as Eliade says, of the "abolition of all norms" and of the "overturning of all values. The very locus appropriated to orgies among primitive peoples, preferably at the critical moments of the harvest (when the seed was buried in the ground), confirms the symmetry between the dissolution of the form (here the seed) in the soil and that of social forms in the orgiastic chaos."[3] Similar ideas and customs are found in many religions. It seems that some customs connected with Halloween even in our day remind us of this.

From time immemorial India has believed in the existence of an all-embracing world order. Even the old Vedas mention a certain *rta,* a power that controls the whole universe and makes life possible on earth. *Rta* causes the rivers to stream; because of *rta* the sky is colored red every morning. But this same *rta* is the giver of the moral norms to which man is subjected. Of course these norms become evident when man sacrifices, because these holy rituals express the secret of the cosmos. Every act in the sacrificial ritual, even the seemingly most unimportant, has its meaning. The smallest error can make the sacrifice invalid, indeed, make a dangerous power of it. Therefore it is a primordial demand in the sacrificial ritual that man knows *rta* and its commands, and obeys them. A Brahman has this knowledge and can safely perform the act. *Rta* itself is an impersonal power. It is, however, supported and guaranteed by Varuna. Varuna is the god who is thought to be continually in connection with *rta.* He is therefore implored

---

[2] Gerardus van der Leeuw, *Phänomenologie der Religion,* 2nd ed. Tübingen: Mohr, 1956, p. 182.
[3] Eliade, *The Myth of the Eternal Return,* pp. 68f.

to forgive sins. In the Rig-Veda we find the following moving prayer:

> When will I be able to approach Varuna again? What sacrifice will he accept from me without wrath? When will I behold his compassion with joy? I seek my sins, Varuna, I long to know them.

Besides *rta*, there is also *dharma*. The literal meaning of this word is "that which is established or firm, steadfast." The word *dharma* is also used to indicate that the cosmos displays itself as a harmonious entity, with everything in its right place and with its own characteristics. The *dharma* of water is its downward flow; the *dharma* of fire and smoke, however, is their upward movement. *Dharma* also concerns the relationship between the different groups of creatures, and since humanity is also divided into different groups or castes, it is natural that *dharma* especially settles the relationship between these castes. That is how the word *dharma* came to play such an important role in the social life of India. Every caste has to stick to its own *dharma;* it has to interpret the essence of its being. If the Brahman is true to his calling and acts according to his *dharma,* and if the Kshatriya follows his instructions, in short, if every caste behaves in accordance with its *dharma,* then society remains calm and peace exists in the world. This specific function of *dharma* has kept India in a sharply defined social pattern. The so-called *varnashramadharma,* i.e., the duties of caste and order, have been the backbone of the life of the people in India for centuries. That these duties were so influential is because the difference between the castes was regarded as having been founded in prehistoric times. The tenth Rig-Veda volume describes how in prehistoric times the mythical giant Purusha was sacrificed by the gods. From his head the Brahmans were born, from his arms the Kshatriyas, from his shanks the Vaishyas and from his feet the Shudras. That is why the difference between the castes, and the *dharma* connected with them, is so extremely important. Another well-known

conception, closely related to *dharma,* is *karma.* The literal
meaning of this word is "work, the effect of an action." In
India's religious literature it has gradually come to mean an
automatically working law, which causes the once-committed
deed to entail unavoidable evil consequences. The committed
evil punishes itself. The *karma* haunts man and decides his
fate. Because it surpasses death, it causes a person who has not
lived according to the *dharma* to re-enter the world after his
death, but this time in a lower position, for he must pay for
the misdeeds of his previous existence. In a certain sense
karma binds men to their past and thus oppresses them; on
the other hand, however, it urges them to conduct themselves
conscientiously, according to their *dharma,* so that they retain
their moral level. Thus considered, we can say that *karma* al-
lows men to make their own choice and to leave them free to a
certain extent. To give an example: a poor beggar, who by
begging for alms makes it clear that by helping him others
improve their *karma* and become happier, has this view of life.

Thus Hinduism confronts mankind with the great realities
of *dharma* and *karma* and consequently with the necessity of
norms. On the other hand, it also seems to have a vague notion of a "beyond," a sphere above and beyond the norm. In
the physical world (*vyaktam*) the norm is necessary to maintain the relationship between the castes. The world would be
a chaos without the norm, and human society would simply
be impossible. But the man who through asceticism or surrender to the gods is elevated above the boundaries of human society and returns to the nonphysical, formless state of the very
first beginning is automatically freed from the rules govern-
ing the lives of others. India's epic writings relate stories of
godlike heroes who tower high above the everyday human affairs. They tell us about religious ecstatics who were completely overpowered by the spell of the gods. Such people were not
subject to the standards of human morals. They had left the
varnashramadharma far beneath them.

Owing to the fact that Buddha painstakingly avoided all

cosmological speculations and concentrated solely on the way to salvation, the norm occupies a very important place in Buddhism. It is not as closely related to the structure of the cosmos as in Hinduism and also misses the important social aspect dominant in the latter. Theravada Buddhism has no castes and consequently no *varnashramadharma,* but it advocates a norm belonging to the noble eightfold path. This norm demands of the pupil that he abstains from killing, stealing, sensuality, lying and intoxicating liquors or drugs. The ultimate objective of *dharma* is to be freed from the fascinating power of this vain world. Man must disengage himself; he must conquer all his passions and thus come to the redeeming insight of the vacancy, the *anatta*-state of this world. In this conception the norm no longer has any cosmological roots but is entirely integrated in the mystic-ascetic ideal of separation from the world.

The religion of China emphasizes the cosmic order. This order, the divine (and bisexual) *tao,* dominates the world in all its aspects and is the origin of all things. In oracular language it is said of *tao*: "Tao . . . I know not whose son he is. He appears to precede the Sublime Lord (Shang-ti). The *tao* is concealed and nameless and yet she is great and giving and fulfilling." The *tao* causes the successions of the seasons in calm rhythm, but it is she who establishes the boundaries and norms in our human society. She has ordered everything in it and has given everybody his own place. The sovereign must act as is becoming to him, while the subject must conduct himself according to his station in life. Every group, every class has its own system of duties. And *tao* controls all of them.

Chinese literature is full of wise lessons concerning *tao.* For instance, a butcher who keeps the *tao* knows that he has to cut the meat in a certain way; that he may not cut it any way he likes but only exactly between the joints. If he does this his work is easy, because it is in conformity with *tao.* When one wants to drive a nail into the wall one must carefully select a suitable place. If one does one has no difficulties, because one follows the *tao*. But when one hits the nail any which way, and consequently not according to the *tao,* then one loses some of the *tao*. Human pride often prevents men from listening to the whispering voice of *tao*. This is the way Chinese Hinduism has formulated the secret of *tao* and ascribed to her the origin of the moral laws which govern society.

Islam has a totally different conception of the norm. It does not base the norm on a cosmic order. The law was given by Allah and must therefore be respectfully obeyed. In Moslem theology this law has been developed into its smallest details. The theocratic point of view, so essential in Islam, automatically controls all theological thinking. To understand this divine law is considered to be of the utmost importance, not only for the happiness of the individual but also for the welfare of the state. The Islamic states, e.g., Pakistan, Arabia, and others, are greatly concerned to make constitutions which agree with the law given by Allah himself.

Already in the early history of Islamitic theology people wondered what the backgrounds were of the distinction between good and evil, beautiful and odious. Why was one thing good and another bad? The most obvious answer was, of course, that all the commandments of Allah are good, but everything he had forbidden is bad. When Islam came in touch with Greek philosophy and involuntarily underwent its influence, however, this answer no longer seemed satisfactory. So a new interpretation was given, namely, that Allah had commanded a certain thing because it was good. For the law of Allah only expressed what was fixed by virtue of logical necessity right from the very beginning, and what could be accepted by human understanding.

For some time Moslem thinking was charmed by this thought which was defended by some of the Mutazilites. But it was not long before its dangers were detected, namely, rationalism and abstract reasoning, which could easily supplant a genuine belief in the trustworthiness of Allah's word. Therefore orthodox

Islam, strongly opposed to these suppositions, continually emphasized Allah's holy will as the only ground for distinguishing between good and evil. Allah had revealed his holy will, and men could find it out. When reflecting upon this the theologians came to the conviction that the *fikh* had four roots, and consequently four sources 'from which men can learn Allah's will. First and foremost is, of course, the Koran itself, which clearly reveals the will of Allah. Further, there is the *hadith*, which describes the conduct of the prophet, also of great importance. The prophet's own example is a kind of mirror from which men can learn Allah's commandments. In the third place there is the *ijma*, the concord of the four great theological schools which developed in Islam. Finally there is the logical inference by analogy to give men insight into their duties towards God.

In all these religious systems, the norm is religious. The moral norm is rooted in divine commandments and belongs to a divine world order.

In Greece another trend of thinking developed which tried to found the moral norm differently. Especially in the days of the sophists Socrates and Plato, virtue, *arete,* was much talked about. The word *arete* itself originally meant "prominence." Etymologically it is related to the Indian idea of the *arya,* the nobleman. Later on Greek thought was preoccupied with the question of which was the most important virtue. The virtue of *sophia* (wisdom), characteristic of the leading class, the governors of the state, was given the highest place. The second place went to *andreia* (virile courage), belonging to the second class, the guardians, the military power in charge of order. The third went to *sophrosune* (thoughtfulness), typical of the ordinary citizens. When all the different classes of society "did their share" (*ta eauta prattein*) it was called *dikaiosune,* "just, harmonic order." In a just society the interests of all the groups are in balance, and hence there is peace and prosperity.

Although this Greek conception of the four virtues can be said to show something of a cosmic order, the word *arete* is man-centered and has very little religious connotation. Perhaps that is why the Greek New Testament seldom uses the word (cf. Phil. 4:8; II Peter 1:3, 5). The Greeks' answer to the question how we can get to know the norms of good and evil, was that they were inherent in our nature. They were part of our being human; we could awaken them by remembering them and by being conscious of them. In the humanism of later centuries this idea was further developed. Humanism said that moral norms are inherently known; we cannot change them at will. Although they govern our lives, they nevertheless originate from us. These norms, this system of values, is clothed in mystery. We must not violate them, and as soon as we ignore them, we are no longer really man.

The Norm and Its Problems

Let us try to give a resumé of our investigation and examine the results more closely. It is evident that the moral norm is an integral element in every religion all over the world. The norm has religious roots, but we meet great differences as soon as we ask where these roots must be sought.

We saw that in primitive religion there is a vague notion of a cosmic order, created in prehistoric times by a High God who put an end to the original chaos. This cosmic order settled the relations within the tribe and prescribed the rules for marriage, which must be obeyed. This norm with her numberless coercive regulations was handed down by the ancestors and demands absolute adherence. Every now and then the original situation of primeval ages returns, as it were, and then for a little while these rules do not apply. So there is a "beyond"; sometimes men can escape the grasp of the norm.

In Hinduism the norm is based on the distinction between the castes and the specific place and task which each occupies in society. Each caste has its characteristic *dharma*. This *dharma* is not a human invention but has divine authority because it originates from primeval ages. Sometimes the *dharma* seems strange and cruel. In one of the best-known products of

Indian literature, because the Kshatriya Arjuna is forced by *dharma* to fight his own relatives in a cruel war, he revolts at it. The god himself appears to him as his charioteer and shows him that he simply must fulfill his divine *dharma,* and that he need not worry about the misery he will cause because it all is part of the vanity of this world:

> Knowing it birthless, knowing it deathless, knowing it endless,
> Forever changing
> Dream not you do the deed of the killer,
> Dream not the power is yours to command it.
> Not wounded by weapons, not burned by fire, not dried by
>   the wind,
> Not wetted by water
> Such is the Atman.[4]

Arjuna can avoid the battle, but it is better for him to fulfill the *dharma* without expecting reward and only to obey his Lord. In Hinduism there is also a conception of a beyond. Sometimes the world returns to the chaotic state of affairs as it was in prehistoric times. But the wise man, he who has transcended his own passions and selfishness, is no longer bound by the ties and rules of this world. He can do the things others cannot do because they no longer affect and infect him.

Buddhism, in its original form, based the norm specifically on the necessity of dissociation. Man must loosen himself from this vain world if he is to be free. The noble eightfold path demands a complete freedom from passions.

In Buddhism there is also a consciousness of a heavenly realm, the heart of the cosmos, where *tao* has unlimited power. In some respects Chinese thinking is sociocentric, but the whole concept of society life is based on religious views.

In Islam the norm is not based on an all-absorbing cosmic order but it is directly attributed to Allah. It may be true that in formulating this norm social aspects such as the consent of the group (the *ijma*), and reason, played a part, but fundamentally this norm results from Allah's sublime will.

---

4 Bhagavad Gita, p. 37.

Finally we saw that in Greek philosophy the norm is thought to originate in man in some way or other. It awakes in man, is born in man, and is connected with the greatest mystery of his existence.

In all these ideas we find that man is very conscious of the fact that the norm has binding and religious authority which he cannot escape.

THE NORM AND FREEDOM

In life we are confronted with a norm that demands obedience. Yet somehow this demand implies a certain freedom. Apparently we are free creatures who can obey or disobey. However, the very supposition of freedom confronts us with another problem. It is a remarkable problem because the idea of "law" used in nearly all languages for the religious and moral norm is also used for the so-called "law" of nature. The "law" of gravity does not ask me if I want to fall or not; it takes me along whether I like it or not. The Hindu idea of *rta* means in the first place the cosmic order, the order of nature. *Rta* makes the sun to rise every morning and to set at evening. There is no escaping from it. *Rta* also forms the basis of the moral and religious demands to which man is subjected. The Greek word *nomos,* and our word *law,* are characterized by the same ambiguity. It is used for what is considered to be a law of nature which cannot be disobeyed, but also for the commandment which demands obedience. If we regard language as a means of expressing a common human consciousness we can infer from the word *law* that man first of all felt himself part of the cosmos, and subject to the cosmic order. That is why he did not consider himself a unique being in this cosmos. We could turn it round and say that man intuitively felt that because water always streams downward, smoke always goes upwards, the sun rises every morning, all these things obey the cosmic order of their own free will and thus give him an example. At any rate, here we touch upon the great human mystery — "both man's involvement in nature and his transcendence over it," his being "<u>involved in both</u> <u>freedom and necessity</u>."[5] While man's religious consciousness makes him realize that he belongs to the cosmic community, the family of creation, the norm confronts him with the mystery of his existence, his freedom and responsibility. Religious consciousness contains a certain tension. Every religion has such a tension between man's passivity and activity, between his lack of freedom in the rhythm of cosmic events and his responsibility.

Albert Schweitzer, the well-known missionary of Lambarene, speaking of the difference between the Christian faith and other religions, said in one of his books:

> All problems of religion, ultimately, go back to this one — the experience I have of God within myself differs from the knowledge concerning Him which I derive from the world. In the world He appears to me as the mysterious, marvellous creative Force; within me He reveals Himself as ethical Will. In the world He is impersonal Force, within me He reveals Himself as Personality. The God who is known through philosophy and the God whom I experience as ethical Will do not coincide. They are one; but how they are one, I do not understand. Christianity must clearly and definitely put before men the necessity of a choice between logical religion and ethical religion, and it must insist on the fact that the ethical is the highest type of spirituality, and that it alone is living spirituality. Thus Christianity shows itself as the religion which, penetrating and transcending all knowledge, reaches forward to the ethical, living God, who cannot be found through contemplation of the world, but reveals Himself in man only.[6]

5 Reinhold Niebuhr, *The Nature and Destiny of Man,* Vol. I. London: Nisbet, 1945, p. 193.

6 Albert Schweitzer, *Christianity and the Religions of the World.* Tr. by Johanna Powers. N. Y.: George H. Doran, 1923, pp. 83, 91.

CHAPTER V

BETWEEN ACTIVITY AND PASSIVITY

The average man does not often think about the strange riddle of his existence. As a rule he just lives on, but sometimes it suddenly strikes him that life seems to have two sides, an active and a passive side, and that it is extremely difficult to draw a boundary line between them. The following example will make this clear. I cannot say, "I beat my heart" or "I make my heart beat," because the beating of my heart belongs to the passive side of my life. I have no control over it; I cannot stop or start my heart beating through using my will. Hence the word "I" cannot be used in this connection. But I can say, "I breathe," for nature has given me a small amount of freedom in this respect. I cannot possibly stop breathing — my freedom is not as great as that — but I can breathe quickly or slowly, deeply or lightly. And because nature has left me this choice we can use the word "I" in this connection. I cannot say, "I digest my food." Digestion belongs to the passive side of my existence; but it is possible to say, "I eat." There again nature has given me a little freedom. I cannot refuse to eat; my freedom does not go that far. But I can eat what I choose. When we regard our lives from this point of view we realize that we are intimately related to nature, of which we are a part, but that some areas of free choice have been entrusted to us. Where this freedom appears, the word "I" has a legitimate place.

It would be interesting to examine which things belong to the active side of life and which to the passive side. At a glance it is obvious that very many things belong to the passive side of our existence. First, there are the country in which we were born and the nation to which we belong. We have not chosen these ourselves, but they were given us at our birth. Second, there are our parents, with their own character, talents and intellect. It stands to reason that these things play an important role in our own lives, because they determine the hereditary base of our lives. In this connection we mention our dispositions, our aptitudes, our intellectual capacities, our physical constitution, and so forth.

We must also mention the education we received in our childhood. Research has shown how significant the experiences in our early childhood can be for the future. But we have not chosen this education ourselves; it was given us. The same is true with regard to the surroundings in which we grew up, the neighbors and friends we lived among, the teachers who trained us; and many more examples could be given.

Undoubtedly the passive side of life is very important and decisive. And this process continues as long as we live. When we are grown up there are numberless passive factors that burden or benefit us — the character of our employers, the qualities of our fellow workers, or our rivals, and sometimes very ordinary incidental events which we call fortunate or unfortunate — all help to shape our lives.

On the other hand there is the active side of our lives. It is easy to point out where that begins. It is found in my response from the cradle on to what fate confronts me with. It is that which I myself shape from all that fate thrusts upon me. It is impossible to indicate exactly where "I" reigns; we can never analyze it psychologically, it retreats as soon as we think we have found it. But one thing is sure: every person is conscious that he does something with and gives an answer to the many factors that shape his life. We have purposely talked about this matter of activity and passivity only in a very general way, but it is clear that it has particular religious roots. Man's religious consciousness has always been confronted with the subtle relationship between activity and passivity in his life.

From the outset it strikes us that the religions which teach that man is but an atom in the immense universe at the same time emphasize the fate-side, the passivity of life. According to this teaching we are only tiny particles carried along by the rolling waves of the cosmos. Our greatest illusion is that we imagine ourselves to be an "I," and so we keep aloof from the cosmos, whereas in reality we are totally submerged by it and are part of it.

Whenever this idea prevails no justice can be done to the active aspect of life. We have already noted, in a preceding chapter, that for this reason it is difficult to find a place for the moral norm and its appeal to our responsibility in the framework of a religion that only sees man in relation to the cosmic reality.

In the ancient religions of Mesopotamia, man was still very much regarded as a small part of the cosmic family. The ancient thinkers of Mesopotamia came to the conclusion that there is a certain "correspondence" between the earthly sphere to which we belong and the heavenly sphere whose full majesty is displayed by the stars. This implied in the first place that the Mesopotamians' temples must be built according to the pattern of the cosmic temple — or "in accordance with the writing of the sky."[1] But on the basis of the correspondence or analogy between the two spheres of heaven and earth they also built their science of astrology, which holds that what happens on earth is a reflection of events in heaven. Because heaven takes precedence over the earth, the events are first outlines in the heavenly regions. As Kristensen states, "There is a parallelism

---

[1] W. Brede Kristensen, *The Meaning of Religion*. Tr. by John B. Carman. The Hague: Nijhof, 1960, p. 52.

between heaven and earth: the heavenly bodies, the planets, guide the earthly events and God guides the heavenly bodies." Thus is "the religious theory of a parallelism between heavenly and earthly events worked out in a natural philosophy and natural science which applies this theory to particular events."[2] This idea has played a very important role in the history of Mesopotamia. The authors of *Before Philosophy* say that "in Mesopotamia the assembly of the gods assigned a mere mortal to rule men, and the divine favor might at any time be withdrawn from him. Man was at the mercy of decisions he could neither influence nor gauge. Hence the king and his counsellors watched for portents on earth and in the sky which might reveal a changing constellation of divine grace, so that catastrophe might be foreseen and possibly averted."[3] We might call this idea the astral conception of man's place in the cosmos. Man is part of the immense cosmic universe, which consists of two corresponding spheres. It is only natural that this idea should now tend towards fatalism. Of course man's activity and responsibility in life assert themselves occasionally, but in his world view in general the feeling of being a victim predominates. In the midst of this mysterious universe he is merely a powerless creature who must bow to fate.

In India we find a quite different situation. To be sure, there, too, man is considered a cell in the great body of the cosmos. But Hinduism considers this idea to be the very essence of man. Man is a microcosmos in the midst of the cosmos in which all the cosmic powers are concentrated and manifested. Hinduism does not emphasize the astral aspect but has a keener eye for the strange phenomenon that *devas* and *asuras,* gods and demons, heroes and giants, the forces of order and chaos, which carry on a continuous war in the whole universe, are also found in human society and in every individual. Consequently, Hinduism must come to grips with the fate-side of life. It

2 *Ibid.,* p. 229.
3 Henri Frankfort, H. A. Frankfort, et al., *Before Philosophy*. Harmondsworth, England: Penguin Books, 1951 (Pelican Book), p. 240.

holds that we *are lived* more than we *do live* in a purely active sense. To live is in the first place to be carried along by the mighty stream of the cosmic process, although we sometimes show a powerless resistance here and there. The fatal impotence of man is movingly depicted in the "lamentations of Draupadi," part of the great epic, the Mahabharata. When the Pendavas are exiled and great misery befalls them, Draupdi, no longer able to control himself, addresses the chief of the Pendavas, the noble Yudisthira, as follows:

> O here amongst men, just as a wooden doll is made to move its limbs by the wire-puller, so are creatures made to work by the Lord of all. Ah, Bharata, like space that covereth every object God, pervading every creature, ordaineth its weal or woe. Like a bird, tied with a string, every creature is dependent on God.
> Like a tree, fallen from the bank in the middle of the stream, every creature followeth the command of the Creator, because imbued with his spirit and because established in Him.
> Enveloped in darkness, creatures are not masters of their own weal and woe. They go to heaven or hell, urged by God himself.[4]

In this bitter lamentation the comparison of human life to a tree in the middle of a stream that can follow only the course of the river strikes us particularly. But this lamentation expresses touchingly, too, how man, small as he is and in the grasp of the all-powerful cosmic process, tries to resist, and how difficult it is for him to resign himself to the course of events.

Hendrik Kraemer, in his book *The Christian Message in a Non-Christian World,* has pointed out that the great cultures of East Asia have not produced "anything that belongs to the category of real tragedy, although these civilizations have been so superbly creative in the different branches of artistic ex-

---

[4] *The Mahabharata of Krishna Dwaipayana Vyasa,* Vol. II: Vanaparva, Arjunabhiganana Parva, Section 30. Tr. by Protap Chandra Roy. Calcutta: 1884.

pression." The cause of this is, according to Kraemer, that "tragedy presupposes the mystery of absolute contrasts." Greece produced tragedy, for "the autonomous individual matched himself against fate or the mysterious world order." But Hinduism never saw man as an autonomous individual; it always considered man in his relationship to the cosmic universe and his life as dominated by the cosmic powers. The moving lamentation of Draupadi shows that this conception has been entertained and that a sense of tragedy was not wholly absent in Hinduism.[5]

This consciousness of tragedy in human life, as expressed in the lamentations of Draupadi, is remarkable because it goes back to the vague notion that even the so-called active side of life should be considered part of the passive side. Even that which I think I am doing myself is but the game of fate that controls me. The German poet Friedrich Schiller expressed it as follows: *"Der Zug des Herzens ist des Schicksals Stimme"* ("The impulse of the heart is the voice of destiny"). Thus considered, I am indeed nothing more than a tree floating along on the current, or a wooden doll made to move its limbs by the puppeteer. I have completely ceased being an "I," and keeping aloof from the great cosmic process, I am dissolved in the cosmic totality.

It must be added, however, that Hinduism has always shown a certain reserve in drawing this logical conclusion. True, it admits that human acts are determined by the cosmic powers which govern the world, and that the inescapable power of *karma,* the sediment of our actions in previous lives, is like a monster that keeps hold of us and determines our lives. But Hinduism also holds that there is something so deeply hidden in man that it transcends his thoughts and desires. That innermost something that is not carried along in the whirlpool has all kinds of names. It is his *atman,* his deepest self; it is the silent *sakshin,* the looker-on or witness, who does not partici-

---

[5] Kraemer, *The Christian Message* . . . , p. 154.

pate in the game of life but only watches what is happening. Man is never entirely absorbed by the cosmic process; there is something in him that aspires higher. True, he is a particle in this spectacular world which is marked by contrasts; but at the same time he participates in what was, in the beginning, the prehistoric unity, the divine power from which everything originates.

The Greek concept of tragedy is of an entirely different nature. It feels the absolute irrationality of life as a smarting pain and expresses this in its notion of gods playing their obscure game with us without our knowing the reasons. Even Oedipus did not know that the gods had decided that he should kill his father and marry his mother. As an infant he was abandoned because his father, King Laios, had learned this prophecy. After many years, when Oedipus had become a man, he happened to meet his father. They had a quarrel, and Oedipus killed his father. Then Oedipus became king of Thebes and married a woman who later proved to be his mother. Human self-esteem revolts against this irrational and senseless divine act because it clashes with his deeply-rooted sense of fairness and justice. This clearly shows an entirely different concept from that expressed in the lamentations of Draupadi which render human acts uncertain. It is remarkable how language sometimes can render human acts uncertain. It sometimes employs the passive voice for what is essentially an active deed of man. It does so to express that the subject not only performs but also undergoes the action. The most striking example is the expression "to fall in love." This is one of the most radical acts in human life because the whole of man's person is involved. It is even more remarkable when we consider that nearly all languages use the passive voice for this act. That reminds me of what a student once told me concerning a co-ed: "She is such a nice girl that I have prayed to God that I may fall in love with her." This clearly shows the paradox of passive activity or active passivity.

But there are other instances in which language brings out

subtly the greater or lesser passivity of our deeds. It often uses the important little word "it"; for instance, *it* occurred to me; *it* struck me," etc. It seems as if the language here goes out of its way to show that I am not nearly as active as it perhaps appears. Much stirs inside of me which, in the deepest sense of the word, I do not do myself but which comes over me and, as it were, carries me along. If this is true of the Western languages, which as a rule strongly accentuate human activity and responsibility, it is obvious that this will be even more true of languages of Eastern peoples who generally prefer objective and passive forms in which "I" does not glaringly come to the fore.

The great insoluble problem of the relationship between the active aspect and the passive aspect of life is very evident in Islam. Especially during the first centuries after the hegira this problem occupied its theologians. A question of particular importance was: Does the *qadar,* the divine command, apply to all of human life, the active side included? Are *all* our actions predestined by Allah, and are we ourselves entirely powerless? It cannot be denied that the Koran clearly teaches this predestination in certain texts. Allah himself is called Al Mudill, i.e., "He who leads astray." "Verily God misleadeth whom He will, and guideth whom He will" (35:9). In another sura we find: "Had we pleased we had certainly given to every soul its guidance. But true shall be the word which hath gone forth from me — I will surely fill hell with Djinn and men together" (32:13). It is no wonder that theological reflection on these questions led to serious discussions, which particularly concerned the question if and to what extent man can be called "the originator of his own acts." Is he only an object in the hands of almighty Allah, or is there at least a trace of self-determination and responsibility? The so-called *qadarites* especially emphasized man's self-determination. They realized that a denial of it would easily lead to a slackening of morals, and, as a result of this, a deterioration of society. For that reason they defended the freedom of the human will, because it was they who watched over the welfare of the people. Their argumentation was later adopted and reformulated by the Mutazilites. It is not logical to assume that all of human life, in every respect, is the product of Allah's *qadar*. If it were so, Allah could never punish the sinner righteously. Allah's *adl,* justice, implies that there must be something like human freedom. "Man makes his own choice, he is the originator of his own acts."

We cannot hold it against the theological thinkers of the early centuries of Islam that they were not able to solve this insoluble problem. They struggled with it, and above all passionately defended the complete sovereignty of Allah. This naturally led them to a decisive opinion of human freedom. One of the writings of that century concludes unhesitatingly: "We confess that man, his works, his confession, his knowledge are created. If the doer is created, a fortiori his acts are created."[6] Nevertheless, every now and then the notion of responsibility, and, with it, of some human freedom, returned, but it could not come to full development because the absoluteness of Allah's sovereign will was held to be unquestionable.

Orthodox Islam offered a solution (after a long time of struggle) in the word *kasb,* i.e., acquisition. It is found at the end of the second sura, where the Koran says: "God will not burden any soul beyond its power. It shall enjoy the good which it hath acquired, and shall bear the evil for the acquirement of which it laboured" (II. 286). This is explained to mean that man is ever busy to acquire what Allah has decided for him; he appropriates what Allah has willed. Thus a certain amount of human activity is allowed for. Man is perhaps not the "originator of his acts," but he is the "acquirer of his acts." His acts are at the same time God's acts; they are taken up

---

[6] The Wasiyat Abi Hanifa, quoted in A. J. Wensinck, *The Muslim Creed.* Cambridge: The University Press, 1932, p. 128.

in the divine plan, and so man is not allowed not to appropriate the acts which God determined.

We need not go into these theological problems more extensively. But let us note that in Islam the problem occupies an entirely different place than in those religions which are based on the cosmos and its divine order and laws. The religions of Mesopotamia and India can be reckoned among the latter, as we have seen, but it is obvious that the number of naturalist religions is considerably larger. We have noted that all over the world people in their religious life first of all turned to the cosmos and sought in it an image of divine powers. And because man himself is but a moment in the cosmos, his existence is involved in it from the very beginning.

THE HEART OF THE MATTER

The most important question is how we consider human life. In the ordinary experience of life we get the impression that human existence can be formulated simply as a continuous interplay of fate and act. Man undergoes things; his fate is determined by all kinds of factors, and he reacts upon them — he reacts and responds. But is that possible — can man react and respond? If he can, it somehow implies that although he is only a speck in the cosmos, he has his own place and can resist the powers that threaten to overwhelm his life. It also implies that the word *I* really is significant and not just an illusion. Reinhold Niebuhr says: "Man is the only animal which can make itself its own object. This capacity for self-transcendence which distinguishes spirit in man from soul (which he shares with animal existence), is the basis of discrete individuality, for this self-consciousness involves consciousness of the world as the other."[7]

Indeed, this is where the riddle of man's life begins — with the consciousness of the world as "the other." It belongs to the essence of being human that man has a twofold place in

[7] Niebuhr, *The Nature and Destiny of Man,* I, 58.

the totality of the universe: he is undeniably a particle in the universe, an atom in the immense cosmos, but at the same time there is something in him that transcends the cosmos and enables him to see it as "the other." It is only natural that philosophers have constantly grappled with this fundamental problem of human existence. In antiquity Stoic philosophy concerned itself intensely with it. Later on it was particularly Spinoza who gave it much thought. Because this deep thinker placed himself in the totality, it stands to reason that "the capacity for self-transcendence," and so the word *I* as well, hardly fit in his system. "In nature," he concludes in his *Ethica,* "there is nothing accidental, but the existent and mode of everything are determined by virtue of the essence of the divine nature."[8] And elsewhere he says, "If men could see clearly through the whole order of nature they would find that all things are as necessary as those they meet in mathematics."[9] The reason Spinoza could say this and be satisfied with it was that he was convinced that God, as the ultimate ground and being of the universe, is perfect reason and that we in our deepest being are one with Him. When we learn to live more and more in accordance with our deepest being we shall acquire the *vera libertas,* the true freedom. These are the basic suppositions of Spinoza's philosophy. After him many other philosophers have reflected on this problem.

Meanwhile it is clear that this problem is in essence a religious problem. Human existence itself is at stake. How does man experience and feel his own existence in the totality of this world? What does he experience when he uses the word *I* and by so doing keeps aloof from the world as "the other"? Every religion must somehow come to grips with this problem. As noted before, primitive religion strongly emphasizes that man is a particle in the cosmos, and nothing more. But primitive man, too, will often question if in reality he is not more

8 Baruch de Spinoza, *Ethica,* I, 29.
9 Baruch de Spinoza, *Cogitata Metaphysica,* II, c. 9, 2.

than that and consequently what the real meaning is of the word *I*. The old astral religions of the Middle East defined the place of man in relation to the cosmos, as we have seen. Every religion that takes the mysteries of human existence seriously is automatically forced to find an answer to the fundamental riddle of human nature. When we examine mankind's struggle with this problem we find different reactions. First of all, we see an intuitive protest against the idea that man is only a particle in the cosmic totality. We already observed this tone of protest in the rebellious words of Draupadi when she was in the depths of her grief. She complains that she is just a puppet in the hands of God or a piece of wood floating on the current, but we realize that she protests passionately against this conception — protests in the name of true humanity.

On the other hand, it needs no proof that the idea that we are but puppets in the hands of the gods, or a piece of wood drifting on the water, can have a peculiar charm. It releases us from the oppressive sense of responsibility, in which case life no longer constitutes a dialogue between our acts and the fate that befalls us, but an even and steady process. Everything we think we are doing is but part of that great, propelling process that embraces the whole world. And if life is no longer a dialogue, we have no guilt; what we did we actually did not do ourselves, but it happened *to us*. It is quite understandable that a person who has made a mess of his life and acknowledges that he was a failure will seize upon this idea to escape the gnawing feeling of guilt. The shameful guilt in our lives becomes less shameful when we can excuse it by saying that we did not do it ourselves but that we were carried along by powers greater than we. The Bible expresses this in a surprising way. The first man, after his first sin, answered God: "The woman whom thou gavest to be with me, she gave me of the tree, and I did eat." In these words we already vaguely hear that excuse which has been used over and over again — my sin is really my fate. The Norwegian poet Henrik Ibsen ends his drama of Julian the Apostate with these words: "Erring human soul, if it is true that thou hast to err, then it will surely not be taken ill of thee when the Almighty will judge the quick and the dead." Again it is obvious that we are dealing here with religious problems.

Hinduism has always somehow resisted a too passive view of life by its *karma*. Its belief in the *karma* as an automatic law of justice shows clearly that it holds that man, to a certain extent, is the creator of his own fate. The circumstances under which he is born are the product of the *karma* of previous existences. Man is constantly busy creating his own existence and preparing his future.

But this idea can, in practice, also cause inactivity and resignation to what happens. The *karma* is inevitable. The pain, the blindness, the cares which are the result of my *karma* of previous existences are inescapable; they cannot be taken away, nor *may* they be taken away. It is quite natural that belief in the *karma* at times led people to embrace a fatalistic attitude to life and hardly stimulated a desire in them to change fate. This is not seldom aggravated by the vague notion that all of our complicated life, with all its intricacies, is only a dream of a god who lies on his back and dreams of a world, then wakes up and shakes off his dream. Somewhere in this dream appears my existence, with all its vicissitudes. The *maya,* the bewitching power of the god, makes me imagine that all is serious and real.

Perhaps we can get a better idea of this *maya* by recalling the myth of Narada.[10] Vishnu, who wanted to reveal his *maya* to Narada, took him on a journey. The weather was hot and dry, and when they approached a village Vishnu said to Narada, "Go to the village and fetch me some water." Narada went to a house. He knocked, and the door was opened by a girl of rare beauty. Greatly impressed by her beauty, he forgot Vishnu's order and remained in the house, married the girl, and after

[10] Quoted in Mircea Eliade, *Images et Symboles.* Paris: Librarie Gallimard, 1952, pp. 91f.

the death of her parents became the owner of the farm. Years
went by. Three children were born. Then one day there was
a dreadful torrent which swept the whole village away, and
Narada's wife and three children were swallowed up by the
flood. He himself was washed ashore somewhere in the wilderness. When he came to, the weather was hot and dry again,
and the earth around him was scorched. Then he heard a
voice saying, "My child, where is the water you were going to
bring me? I have been waiting for you for half an hour." Then
Vishnu added, "Do you understand the secret of my *maya*
now?" Hinduism's answer to the question of what the essence
of life is always reveals that it is still under the spell of this
myth.

CHAPTER VI

THIRST AFTER REDEMPTION

Students of comparative religion have sometimes made a distinction between law-religions and redemption-religions. This distinction is justified only if there are indeed some religions in which the idea of redemption predominates, and others which attach far less value to it. But there is not one single religion which does not to some extent concern itself with the problem of redemption. We can easily illustrate this by referring to so-called primitive religion. Even there we find that man has sought salvation.

One of the essential and characteristic features of primitive religion is that it never and nowhere accepts the natural reality merely for what it is. Primitive religion has also been called nature-religion. But so-called primitive man is in no way disposed to accept natural phenomena without further comment. He always tries to lift whatever nature offers him to a higher level by his rites, thereby to make it truly acceptable. An example of this is rice-growing. For centuries several peoples of East Asia have grown their rice in a surprising and admirable way. Rice paddies must be abundantly irrigated. A mountain stream higher up is dammed up against the slope, and the water is sent down through a network of little channels to the paddies. But the people do not dare dam up the stream before they have first satisfied the spirit of the stream by all kinds of rituals on that particular spot. Then the rice is sown on the well-irrigated fields. As soon as the plants have developed a little, the time has come to transplant them in the actual fields. This is usually done by the women, but again not before all sorts of ceremonies have been performed, because man is once more interfering in the course of nature. Both when preparing the fields, and especially at harvest time, old customs must be followed strictly and countless rites obediently performed. For rice is not merely another vegetation, it is a goddess, a heavenly being embodied in rice. And such rice cannot simply be used for food — it must be treated in accordance with her divine nature. What this means is that the simple, natural reality is raised to a higher level, it is made sacred, it is given a quality that makes it beneficial. This lifting up of reality — we might say this redemption — is brought about by rites and ceremonies.

This attitude applies not only to rice. The building of a house requires the same precautions. To these people, a dwelling is not simply a place where men find shelter; it is an image of the world, a microcosmos with a kind of mountain of the gods in the middle. At any rate, a dwelling is a place where man lives together with invisible powers, tutelary spirits, the lares and penates. Consequently various rituals must be performed before first selecting the place and later building the house. But there is more. Even man is not fully man the way nature has made him. All kinds of things must be done to him, too, and often these rites begin long before his birth. Accordingly, the moment he is actually born, the moment he touches mother earth for the first time, in short, at every important moment, *rites de passage* are observed.

Most important of all is the initiation, again attended by all kinds of ceremonies. This even makes a person a fit member of the community. Many peoples practice circumcision, the sign that a man is incorporated in the sacral community. But this is again an instance where the ordinary realities of nature are not accepted as they are. All along the line the actual reality must be made sacred, to have a livable world. To say it in different terms: all along the line the reality given by nature must undergo a "redemption." Only then will it be beneficial. This is the first manifestation of "thirst after redemption" in primitive religion.

The myths of primitive peoples show another aspect deserving our attention. The Dutch missionary Adriani, who worked on the Indonesian island of Celebes for many years, tells some of the myths of the Toradjas who live there. In their myths these people relate that the Lord Creator intended to give man "the long breath," i.e., everlasting life. Unfortunately there was a hostile power, the power of the Night, who gave man, when it was dark, the "short breath," fleeting life, like the wind in the night which only blows a little while and then falls again. That is why man is mortal. A typical feature in this myth is that death was the result of a blunder — the Lord Creator had not quite finished his work before he exposed his creation to threatening, hostile powers. This "blunder" concept is typical of many myths among various kinds of peoples. Long ago, in prehistoric times, the time before all times, something must have happened that caused man's struggle with numberless insurmountable difficulties, and especially death.

These myths express surprise at, and fear of, death. It is the same fear we meet in numberless ancient writings of mankind. We mention only the well-known ancient Gilgamesh epic which expresses this fear in such a moving way. In this ancient Assyrian-Babylonian epic the hero Gilgamesh laments, after his trusted friend Enkidu has died:

> Night and day I bewailed him: I did not bury him: perhaps my friend would rise up at my calling. Thus he lay seven days and seven nights like a worm, fallen on his nose. Since his death I no longer found life. I am like a criminal wandering over the steppe.[1]

---

[1] *The Gilgamesh Epos*, Song 10.

This sadness about "the land from where there is no return" appears to be one of the essential elements in the religious life of mankind. The great mystery of death, its inevitability and finality, have ever fascinated and at the same time frightened man.

In the myths of the Toradjas of central Celebes we find another idea deserving of our attention. They relate that in prehistoric times there was a vine that connected heaven and earth. Along this vine was constant communication between men and the inhabitants of heaven. The former could ascend and the latter descend. One day a celestial being came down and fell in love with a girl on earth. He married her, and a child was born to them. As soon as the celestial being saw that the child had many earthly, human features, he perceived that he could no longer stay on earth. He did not belong there. So he decided to return to heaven, but his wife saw through his plan and climbed up the vine after him, the child in a carrying-cloth on her back. When she had nearly caught up with him he cut the vine so that the woman and her child fell back to earth. But from then on all traffic between heaven and earth was cut off, and man lived his own life without the help of the inhabitants of heaven. Man can no longer ascend. Only a priestess can in a very mysterious way make a journey to heaven, by separating her soul and body; but only for a little while, however, just long enough to fetch some life-breath for someone who is dying. But this is a very dangerous undertaking, which cannot always be carried out.

Thus primitive religion provides a threefold answer to the question of whether mankind feels the need of redemption: (1) Life needs an additional dimension, the dimension of sacredness, to be worth living and beneficial. (2) Life lies under a curse, because in prehistoric times the connection between this world and the celestial world was broken. Therefore there lies a shadow on everything, and nothing reaches its true fullness. (3) Life now is inevitably threatened by death.

It is not difficult to show that these three thoughts have

occupied mankind throughout history. In the first place there
is the great abundance of rites. We still see this among those
peoples whose religion does not occupy a separate place alongside other cultural expressions but absorbs the whole of cultural
life. Among them agriculture itself is a rite; hunting is surrounded by all kinds of religious customs; architecture is a
sacred science; the physician is at the same time a priest and
the priest a physician. In short, every aspect of their life is
religious. Of these cultures we can say that religion gives life
a new dimension and lifts it up above its natural reality. This
additional dimension is not something superfluous, or dispensa-
ble; on the contrary, it gives life safety and stability and welfare. One of the most difficult problems connected with the
present-day rapid diffusion of modern, nonreligious, technical
culture is that its sudden secularization causes a certain unrest,
a strain, and a hidden fear of the future among the primitive nations. They begin to miss the additional dimension, a loss
which cannot always be offset by reasonableness and progress
and democracy. This whole problem reveals man's thirst after
redemption.

The second point is just as clear. In prehistoric times things
happened which brought about a curse on earth. Lasting redemption can be obtained only by an effort to restore the original state of affairs. That is, as becomes more and more evident,
in many cases the deepest meaning of the religious rites. The
rites link men with primeval time. They bring back the blessed-
ness of primeval time. There are primitive peoples who erect
a "tree of life" on solemn occasions which reminds the people
of the dawn of creation. It is stripped of its branches and
leaves to demonstrate that in prehistoric time countless different creatures originated from one tree of life.

All these religious customs indicate that there was a period
of peace and happiness in prehistoric time. It is remarkable
how many peoples are acquainted with some "paradise lost."
Hinduism relates that in prehistoric time this world lived in the

so-called *krta-yuga,* "the age of *krta,*" the age of welfare and harmony, when the commandments were given to maintain life. Unfortunately that golden age is long since past. Other *yugas* have passed, and at present we live in the *kali-yuga,* the "black age," in which all kinds of signs of injustice and chaos begin to reveal themselves. But prehistoric time is always present in the religious rites, in the sacrifices, in the holy proverbs (*mantra*), and we can stretch out our hands to reach for its bliss.

Ancient Egypt interpreted this idea in a remarkable way. It believed that in prehistoric time the "primeval hillock" originated from the primeval waters (*nun*). This hillock was the very first beginning of the world and life. It is still present because it is represented in the temples. But a temple is more than that. It is at the same time the important point of the universe, usually referred to as *akhet,* that point of the eastern horizon where every morning the sun rises triumphantly between two mountains. These mythical mountains are represented as two lions with their backs to each other, or as two high trees. The old tradition had only one *akhet,* the *akhet* of the East. Not until later a corresponding point in the western horizon was added, the point where the sun sets, the western *akhet.* It is quite obvious that this *akhet* plays a very important part in Egyptian religion. It is the crucial point in the cosmos where Rē, the sungod, who sinks in the west in the evening, rises every morning again in glory. This mysterious point makes yesterday and today, past and future, death and life, meet. There the new day is born and all the secrets of life are focused. *Akhet* is also present in the temple. Queen Hatshepsut says in one of her records about the temple of Karnak: "I know that Karnak is the *akhet* on earth." The entrance of the temple itself, the pylon, "is the gate of the world, which means the place of contact and transition from this world to the other world"; it represents the *akhet.* He who enters the temple enters into the greatest secret of the cosmos and passes the boundaries between life and death.[2] Moreover, we must not forget that this *akhet* is the point where once, in prehistoric time, the sun rose for the first time between the mountains. In other words, every person who enters the temple ascends the primeval hillock and stands in the *akhet,* in the dawn of creation. Thus Egyptian religion expressed the belief that in whatever age we may live, primeval time with its life-giving secrets is still with us.

When we go deeper into these things, it appears that in several religions the idea of redemption is intimately connected with other conceptions. Some notion of a "paradise lost" glimmers through, a memory of the distant past of things real in mythical primeval time which can now be made real, in a certain way, in the present. Eliade has rightly pointed out that redemption in many cases implies an "abolition of profane time, of duration, of history, and he who reproduces the exemplary gesture (the priest who performs the holy rites) thus finds himself transported into the mythical epoch in which its revelation took place."[3] Indeed, the idea of redemption and the longing for redemption include wanting to escape history and its fatality, for which we are no match — the eternal return!

Closer reflection on these things shows us that the problem of redemption has been approached in different ways in the history of religion. In the first place it is noteworthy that some religions believe that every person must find his own salvation, while other religions emphasize the redemption of the community as a whole.

In Confucianism we note at once the sociocentric approach. There redemption is in the first place restoration of order in the kingdom in such a way that the sovereign is once again sovereign and the subject again subject. The great evil in this world is not that some people have difficulties but that the social as well as the cosmic unity is broken. Not until all

---

2 Kristensen, *The Meaning of Religion,* p. 374.
3 Mircea Eliade, *The Myth of the Eternal Return,* p. 35.

things are harmoniously ordered under the rule of a just emperor, so that everybody is once again in his right place and does his own duty, can we speak of peace and happiness. Of course, in China there has been for centuries, besides this sociocentric approval, the search for individual redemption, especially in Buddhism.

In Hinduism, too, we find both aspects. It tells of just kings in times gone by, and hopes for the restoration of order and peace that reigned in those times. In the well-known Bhagavad Gita, the fascinating dialogue between the hero, Arjuna, and Krishna, his divine counselor, Krishna, who is the incarnation (*avatara*) of god, says:

> When goodness (*dharma*) grows weak, when evil (*a-dharma*)
> increases
>> I make myself a body.
> In every age I come back to deliver the holy,
> To destroy the sin of the sinner,
> To establish righteousness.[4]

There may be a steady decline in every respect in the history of mankind, but it is not hopeless. God returns to earth in periods of decline and demoralization to restore righteousness. This obviously is a social concept.

But besides this, Hinduism has always strongly emphasized individual redemption, which found expression in the longing to shake off the enchantment of this alluring world, to retire into oneself and thus find union with the divinity. Solitary hermits, after having torn themselves away from their families and the turbulent world, applied themselves to *yoga* and strove for perfect silence inside themselves. They, too, wanted to return to prehistoric time, the time which preceded all times, but they wanted to go back even further than the dawn of the origin of all things. They wanted to return to the divinity in his non-manifested, formless condition. This longing was based on the vague notion that this enchanting world with all its

4 Bhagavad Gita, p. 50.

contrasts and tensions, must somehow be an illusion. The magic of *maya* intoxicates us and forms in us an illusion of a multiform world. As soon as man is freed from this intoxication, all contrasts are dissolved and everything is concentrated in the one, impenetrable secret that Brahman exists and that we are in essence one with him.

This mystic trend in India is seen in the Upanishads. For many centuries they have influenced the thinking of numberless people, and even now they are one of the most influential forces there. Mysticism always tends to draw the attention of the individual to himself; he himself must find what none can give him. India's mysticism is no exception to this rule. There, too, salvation is something which the individual must himself acquire.

It is interesting that mankind has always oscillated between these two: collective redemption and individual redemption. Islam definitely emphasizes the former, but Moslem mysticism tends to emphasize the latter. The modern world reveals both of these trends in a secularized form. German national-socialism was a typical attempt at bringing about collective welfare, utopia. Communism also tried from the very beginning for a better world. Especially today, when communism and socialism still have a battle to fight, many adherents long passionately for the future when the victory will be acknowledged and the great peace will begin. Marx and other founders of this movement use many expressions which have an eschatological ring.

But the whole modern world shows a strong yearning for redemption. Many individuals flee from the dull monotony of daily life, from boredom, discontent, cares, and disappointments, to intoxication, or dancing, or whatever offers oblivion. From the bars and dance-halls of our modern world we hear as a stifled cry the *miserere* of people who see no real meaning in life. Although this yearning for redemption no longer has religious overtones, it is nevertheless present in our world and it is still expressed in the same way.

The second distinction we must make when speaking of redemption is between autosoteric and heterosoteric attempts at redemption. In the first instance man, and man alone, tries to bring about his redemption. In the second instance man expects redemption as a gift from a deity. These two attempts are found side by side in the history of religion. Sometimes they are combined (or in any case come close together); in other religions they are strictly separated. We can say that it is the essence of religious man in his distress and fear to seek help from a divine power. In a number of religions we indeed find it thus. Even primitive man, no matter how primitive he may be, expects redemption from his god or from his ancestors. The prophets of Baal cried to their god to listen to them and to redeem them (I Kings 18:26). But on the other hand, we find in most religions that man at the same time tries to make himself worthy of the favor of his gods by his devotion, his prayers, his obedience, and his sacrifices. Thus he plays a rather important part in his own redemption. When this cooperation is strongly emphasized, redemption is soon regarded as a fruit of man's own labor.

Hinduism, which, as we have seen, occupied itself more than other religions with the problem of *moksha,* redemption, distinguishes between different *margas,* "ways," which men can take. The most common way is the *karma-marga,* the way of dutiful service to the gods, of sacrifices and purifications. Beside this *karma-marga* is the *jnana-marga,* the way of the *gnosis,* of higher knowledge, by which man can come to the redeeming insight of his union with the deity. The third way is the *bhakti-marga,* the way of surrender to, trust in, and love of the divinity. This way is clearly taught in the Bhagavad Gita which we mentioned before, and is regarded as the way which leads to absolute redemption. Krishna, the incarnation of the divinity, says to Arjuna, his pupil:

> Quickly I come to those who offer me every action,
> Worship only Me, their dearest delight,
> With devotion undaunted.

> Because they love Me, these are my bondsmen
> And I shall save them from mortal sorrow
> And all the waves of Life's deathly ocean.[7]

Here we again see belief in divine mercy, which is further expressed in hymns. The divine being that had become more and more a vague, impersonal idea in India's philosophic schools became once again the living Lord, Ishvara, to whom one can pray and of whom one can expect redemption.

We can find a similar development in Buddhism, for Buddha himself seems to have emphasized strongly man's own effort. In his farewell address he spoke to his young followers:

> Therefore, O Ananda, be ye lamps unto yourselves. Rely on yourselves and do not rely on external help. Hold fast to the truth as a lamp. Seek salvation alone in the truth. Look not for assistance to any one besides yourselves.[6]

But it cannot be said that in Theravada Buddhism, which strictly follows the teachings of the master, salvation is considered only the work of man himself. The law of *karma* means that man will himself reap what he has sown, and that he must pass through depths of misery because of his own faults. This implies that the mysterious supreme direction of his life contains a hidden pedagogy, driving him as it were to happiness. It may be true that man must rely only upon himself, but when looked at from a wider perspective there are powers that lift him up. In this sense we might say that Buddhism is not wholly autosoteric. The belief that man does not redeem himself but finds redemption outside himself developed in Buddhism after several centuries. It spread in Mahayana Buddhism, and was embraced especially in Japanese Buddhism, which gave it theological expression.

Japanese Buddhism distinguishes between *jiriki,* salvation by one's own endeavor, and *tariki,* salvation through another's

[5] *Ibid.,* p. 98.
[6] *The Teachings of the Compassionate Buddha.* N. Y.: Mentor, n.d. (Mentor Religious Classic) , p. 49.

power. *Jodo-shin-shu,* a theological trend in this Buddhism, teaches *tariki* with great emphasis. Amitabha (in Japanese, Amida Butsu) vowed that he never wanted to reach the highest enlightenment of the perfect bliss before he knew for certain that all who invoked him and mentioned his name reverently would be saved; thus it is possible for man to enter the Pure Land of bliss by trusting in this vow. So it is not necessary to do a single thing oneself. One of the teachers of this school, Honen, said: "Even a bad man will be received in Buddha's Land, how much more a good man," but another teacher, Shinran, had the courage to turn this around and say, "Even a good man will be received in Buddha's Land, how much more a bad man."[7] The accent no longer lies on man and his work but wholly on Buddha's promise. "Just as a great stone, if on a ship, may complete a voyage of myriads of miles over the waters, and yet not sink, so we, though our sins are heavy as giant boulders, are borne to the other shore by Amida's primal vow."[8]

It is most difficult to pass judgment on this trend in Japanese Buddhism. Whereas H. Haas was inclined to regard it as a duplicate of Christianity in Buddhist garb, Hendrik Kraemer is of the opinion that the *tariki* of the *Jodo-shin-shu* "in reality remains a *jiriki*." The belief in the vow of Amida Buddha is likewise the work of man, but it is just "an easier way" and "a means to work salvation."[9] Karl Barth, when speaking of this form of Japanese Buddhism, makes the following comparison: "One is reminded of Pharaoh's magicians (Ex. 7) who could likewise perform the wonders of Aaron, the brother of Moses; imitating them so closely that it gave Pharaoh occasion to harden his heart."[10]

---

[7] Christmas Humphreys, *Buddhism.* Harmondsworth, England: Penguin Books, 1951 (Pelican Book), p. 163.

[8] Tasuku Harada, *The Faith of Japan.* N.Y.: Macmillan, 1914, p. 95.

[9] Kraemer, *The Christian Message* . . . , p. 180.

[10] Karl Barth, *Kirchliche Dogmatik,* Vol. I, sec. 2. Munich: Kaiser, 1932, pp. 375f.

And so these two ideas emerge again and again in the religions of mankind. In times of oppression the conviction prevails that men must receive redemption and that divine powers alone can give it. But at other times man asserts that it is his own business and that he must bring about his own salvation — *jiriki* and *tariki!* "Be ye lamps unto yourselves," and "Amida Buddha, our refuge!" Indeed, the cry for redemption runs through the history of religion as a groan — but redemption of what?

We have already noticed in primitive religion that life must have an additional dimension. Life in itself is drab, monotonous, unsafe, lusterless; it must become sacred, holy, safe, protected. Throughout all the centuries men have felt deeply and with horror the threatening of death. India dreamed of *amrta,* living water, which could save men from death, and Greece had its *ambrosia.* Life on earth is surrounded by dangers on every side. It is quite natural that the thirst for redemption plays such an important part in history.

It is remarkable that sometimes the idea arises that what we must be delivered from is hidden deeply inside us. India has especially felt this. Man's *ahamkara,* his strong self-esteem, his being so much attached to his own desires, his passions, are the great enemies from which he must be delivered. The evil is not without but within. We must be delivered, Buddha says, from the suffering necessarily connected with our existence in this world, the suffering originating from our fundamental ignorance (*avidya*) and our driving desires. We must be delivered from our "I," mysticism of all ages says. "Hell is where thou art and Paradise where thou art not," one of the Moslem mystics said. It is obvious that he meant "there is no Hell but selfhood, no Paradise but selflessness."[11] "Evil is thou and the worst evil is thou when thou knowest it not."[12]

It is fascinating to observe how mankind has wrestled with

11 R. A. Nicholson, *Studies in Islamic Mysticism.* Cambridge: University Press, 1921, p. 64.

12 *Ibid.,* p. 53.

the problem of redemption throughout the ages. The thirst after redemption has always been there, but as soon as the question arose of what the meaning of redemption was and in which way it must be brought about, there emerged a great variety of ideas. It seems that man has had a vague notion all through the ages that there is something undefinable, something we cannot name, resting on human life and weighing it down, and that there must be salvation available in some way or other.

CHAPTER VII

THE GREAT UNKNOWN IN THE BACKGROUND

It may seem strange that only now, after we have examined the various elements of the different religions, we are going to discuss man's faith in God, or gods, and his relation to Him or them. For various reasons, however, it is necessary to form a clear idea of man's ideas concerning the world and man before we can understand the place God or the gods occupy in these religions. Faith in God, or in gods, is undoubtedly one of the most central aspects of the religions of mankind. Somehow man always appears to have been moved forward, or called back, to this belief, which sometimes disappears almost entirely behind human self-confidence, but as soon as dark days dawn or life becomes uncertain it emerges out of the depths of the human heart and reasserts itself. The history of religion teaches that man and his gods have come a long way, a way of manifold experiences. There have been gods who were worshipped passionately by numberless people but who were completely forgotten by later generations and superseded by other gods. Images of certain gods have been broken to pieces when it became too clear that praying to them was useless. Other gods have been merged in surprising theocracies so that the old figures could hardly be recognized. Still other gods have faded to abstract conceptions in which man still believes but from whom he does not expect any help. In short, much has happened, and all kinds of variations have developed in the long history of man and his gods.

When we examine how man imagined his gods and how he tried to know them, we see in the first place that man deduced the nature of his gods from the world which surrounded him. He observed nature round about him — heaven and earth, the sun which rises majestically every morning, the moon which fades away and reappears again out of nothing in a mysterious regularity — and from these impressions he formed an idea of his gods. The cosmos was the great picture book in which man read the image of his gods. It is only natural, therefore, that the gods who appear in the history of religion usually have a clear "nature-character." They are connected with very concrete natural phenomena, with night or day, with wind or fire, with growth or withering, with life or death. With these gods man lived; they threatened his life but at the same time sustained it, and he knew himself dependent every moment on these gods.

Another natural result is that the gods whom we meet in the history of the religions of mankind often reveal a remarkable ambiguity. On the one hand, they are persons; they are invoked by man and they can appear to man and speak to him. All kinds of stories and myths are told about the strange works which these gods have done. On the other hand, we often get the impression that they are also impersonal, natural powers. Hinduism shows this ambiguity very strongly. Its adherents bowed in their temples before their god seen as the Ishvara, the Lord, to whom one could speak and who would reveal himself to those who approached him. But at the same time they considered Ishvara, in essence, the hidden power which bears all and from which all originates. One evening not long ago I stood at the entrance of a temple dedicated to Shiva, in a little town in India. It was an important moment, because for the first time in history the gates of the temple had been opened to the outcasts. When I asked some Hindus in the square in front of the temple to which god this temple was dedicated, they answered, "This temple is dedicated to Shiva, and there is an image of Shiva in the innermost room. But that is only for the sake of the simple people. They need that as a kind of kindergarten instruction. We know that god is not in a temple or in an image, but that he lives in every flower bud and in every tree and that he is the deepest kernel in every man." These words clearly reveal the religious oscillation in Indian life. India builds temples and brings sacrifices of devotion, but at the same time it maintains that its images are only human phantasies and that temples and statues in reality have no significance.

It always remains difficult to imagine what the adherents of the different religions have thought on seeing their statues and hearing their myths. On the one hand, it is probable that many of them really identified the deity with the statue and really thought it to be present in the statue. On the other hand, we must suppose that most of them knew very well that the identity was not to be taken too literally. The same god represented here in one statue was represented elsewhere in other statues. Although the people did not always realize this, perhaps, they must have understood vaguely that the deity they worshipped did not coincide with the statue in which he was thought to be present. In many myths the real dwellingplace of the deity was heaven, or a high mountaintop in the unapproachable distance.

Probably the relation between the deity and the specific natural phenomenon with which he was thought to be most intimately connected was regarded in the same way. He was identical to it, he was the sun or the wind or fire, but that did not mean that he was only this physical phenomenon itself. In ancient Egypt Rē was already in early times one of the great gods. A hymn of the New Kingdom says: "All gods are three:

Amon, Rē and Ptah, who have no equal. His name is hidden
as Amon; he is Rē in his face; Ptah is his body." This indicated the mystery of the nature of the sungod. He is Amon, too,
but as Amon he is hidden. "He is Rē in his face" means that in
this form he appears every morning in the sky, when he chases
away the shadows of the night. Numberless myths are told
about Rē. The kings are invoked as "sons of Rē." And as it
was in Egypt, so it was in all countries where the sun was worshipped as one of the mighty gods. India has many myths
about Surya, the sungod, about his marriage, his children, his
adventures. Greece had stories about Helios. On hearing
these old myths we always notice the same thing: the god worshipped as sungod is really the sun, he is identical to it, he
shows the features of the sun. But he is not only the celestial
body which we see. He can listen to our prayers, he can ful-
minate, and so on. But again, exactly how these people felt is
difficult to describe. Most likely they fell into different groups.
Some may have identified their god with the sun itself, whereas
others — although perhaps unconsciously and unreasoningly
— thought of a sublime, divine person who revealed himself
in the sun. When studying the history of religion we sometimes get the impression that two powers influenced man at the
same time. Man wanted to deduce the names and virtues of his
gods from the cosmos — the cosmos itself was as it were the
countenance of his gods; but at the same time something led
him to feel that the deity itself was different and greater —
somebody to whom he could pray and to whom he had to give
an account. The church father Tertullian once said that if a
heathen is in sudden distress, he suddenly forgets his various
gods and their names and simply says, "If God wills." It is as
if he knows in his heart of hearts that he has not invoked
Jupiter and Saturn and all the other gods, but that there is
only a hidden power at an untraceable distance whose name
he does not know, but who listens to him.[1]

[1] Tertullian, *De testimonio animae*. Chap. Two.

Meanwhile the great religions of mankind show us that the different peoples have indeed deduced the names of their gods from the cosmos. In so-called primitive religion, this is often done in a strange and confused manner. There we meet spirits of nature, of waterfalls, of mountaintops, of trees and plants. Sometimes it is not clear whether such spirits are divine beings or the spirits of ancestors. At any rate it appears that ancestors can manifest themselves in particular natural phenomena and that life and the safety of the tribe are still largely dependent on their interference. In many religions, however, this whole world of spirits is ordered in a particular system. There are spirits which apparently belong to the heavenly powers: they are light and bring prosperity; others are connected with the earth, with darkness, and with the mysterious, life-giving power hidden in the earth. In various primitive religions we can trace a comprehensive philosophy of life which holds that inside the two cosmic unities, heaven and earth, all things are ordered.

This already implies that there are celestial and chthonian gods in primitive religion. They are connected with nature, with heaven, with the sun, often with the moon or with the earth and its secrets. The fact that belief in a Supreme Power or High God who ordered the world and maintains this order is found in various primitive religions has drawn the attention of many scholars. As early as 1898 the Scottish scholar Andrew Lang published *The Making of Religion,* in which he emphasized this phenomenon. He based his findings on the results of the research made by A. W. Howitt, who journeyed through southeast Australia carefully studying the religious life of the native tribes. He found that these aboriginals believed in a Supreme Being, who is the origin of all things. The Kurnai call him Mungan Ngaur — Our Father. The young people are told the secret of this High God when they are solemnly initiated, because it is he who "initiated the rites." A myth tells of Mungan Ngaur that he later "left the earth and ascended to the sky, where he still remains."[2] Other tribes in Australia appeared to know such a Supreme Being as well. In many cases the aboriginals thought of this Supreme Being in a very primitive way. It is remarkable that, although he is associated with the sun, with heaven, and sometimes with thunder, his connection with natural phenomena in general is not great. Also remarkable is that in Africa, among the Bantu tribes, a similar belief in a High God is found.

The Swedish scholar Nathan Soederblom, in a detailed study on the origin of faith in God (*Das Werden des Gottesglaubens*), observes that these high gods in primitive religion, however exalted they may be, have little meaning for everyday life. As a rule no one prays to them, at least not the ordinary members of the tribe. These gods are too far removed, too exalted. Their significance is that they ordered the world in prehistoric time and created the laws to which man is still subjected. Soederblom is of the opinion that the belief of the Chinese in Shang-ti, the supreme god to whom only the emperor is allowed to pray, is an offshoot of the belief in high gods found in primitive religion. Other scholars hold that the significance of the high gods is that they form a sort of basis of security for the cosmic order.

Primitive religion appears to be very complicated. All kinds of tendencies live alongside each other. Most characteristic is the fact that the divine powers which are feared and believed in, often have little of the nature of personal gods. In many cases they are impersonal powers, mysterious, invisible beings. They are *mana,* supernatural power, hidden in things, not only in natural phenomena but also in sounds, words, days, places. The whole world is full of them and happy is he who knows their secret.

Thus we find here too, although perhaps in a somewhat primitive way, the strange uncertainty which is always present in

2 Andrew Lang, *The Making of Religion,* 3rd ed. London: Longmans, Green, 1909, p. 181.

non-Christian religions: Who is God? Is He far away? Is it impossible to come in contact with Him? Is He a High God? Is He near us? Is He in the world in which we live? Is He in nature that surrounds us? Is He identical with the world? And if He is indeed one with nature and identical to it, what is He — a *he* or a *she* or an *it?* Or is He everything at the same time and does it only depend on how we approach Him? This great riddle of all religion appears clearly already in primitive religion.

HE, SHE OR IT!

Again it is Hinduism which manifests this uncertainty most clearly. We have seen that it now invokes god as an Ishvara, a Lord, and then again as Brahman, the deepest being of all being, the hidden, impersonal background of all things. Or, rather, both forms can be used at the same time. The same man can bow before his Ishvara and sacrifice in the temple, and at the same time believe that this is only a "kindergarten" approach and that God Himself pervades the universe as an invisible power. This is mainly due to the fact that the gods of India, even or especially those whose names are mentioned in the Vedas, are less sharply defined than for instance those of Greece. There are, of course, all kinds of myths, particularly those about Indra, who killed the great monster and saved the cows. Many stories are told about him. Likewise later Hinduism has all kinds of myths about Shiva and Vishnu. But all these tales retain a strange mythical vagueness, a queer irreality. The gods are gods; they belong to another world; they live above this earth, because they are exalted. But they are at the same time so close, so much one with nature and included in it, that they can be *grasped,* as it were.

In India, one of the consequences of this idea was an awareness of the riddle of man. It was held that man was a cell in the great body of the cosmos, but it became more and more clear that he was a very important cell, for all the powers of the cosmos were concentrated in him. Hinduism held that the human eye was the representation of the sun, the human breath of Vayu, the wind-god, the human spine of Meru, the world-mountain, the human warmth of Agni and the body fluids of the ocean. Thus all the powers of nature met in man. But that was saying the same as that all gods meet in man. Proceeding from this starting point Hinduism came to the conclusion that just as this great cosmos, with all its conflicting powers, nevertheless shows a profound unity, man, in whom different abilities accumulate, is in essence a unity. The cosmic self, the cosmic *atman,* the *paramatman,* corresponds with man's deepest being, his *atman.*

When the Vedanta worked out this thought as advanced in the Upanishads, Hinduism gradually became more and more convinced that finding God is the same as finding the innermost being of man himself. God is not somebody outside of man, whom he must seek and in whom he takes refuge, but He is the hidden secret inside. This secret is covered with layers, as it were, called *kocas* in the Upanishads. Man is thought of as a bundle of concentric circles. The outermost circle is his body, the material wall around his being. Inside this is his life, the biological cover. But in the center of his being is the secret, the divine spark, which is one with Brahman. Hence seeking God becomes a pilgrimage to the hidden springs of the divine life in one's own soul. Theology becomes psychology. Temple and altar become kindergarten. Prayer becomes introspection (of oneself). God is no longer the Other, who speaks to man and judges him, but He is the foundation on which man rests. In Islamic mysticism it is frequently said that the true *hajj* is the pilgrimage to the true Mekka — the depth of one's own heart. There lies the Kaaba, where time and eternity, Creator and creature meet.

Incidentally, we may mention that the Indian religions could speak of God as the hidden secret within because they believed the *karma* to be the power of requital. The *karma* is automatic and belongs entirely to the realm of the earth. Man reaps what he has sown, and that is so universal that nobody can doubt it. No god appears on the scene to punish sins, no justice to retaliate evil. In the religions of India the divine judgment which other religions place at the end of life, behind the mysterious gates of death, takes place during life, or at least in the series of lives in the course of which man gradually matures for salvation. And Brahman is the origin of all things and at the same time the end in which all is absorbed. Nothing can be said about it, only that it is *neti neti,* neither this nor that, neither masculine nor feminine; it is the still secret which lies behind all things, and from which all originates.

Although this vagueness we have discussed is one of the most striking characteristics of the religions of India, it is also found in other religions. The Chinese religions mention *t'ien,* heaven, again and again. The word may indicate a god, but it is generally used to denote an impersonal power and is almost identical to natural law or simply nature. The word *tao,* which occupies such an important place in Chinese religion, is an impersonal power, too, an *it,* which dominates the world. The history of religion reveals the same vagueness everywhere. The gods are real, personal powers with whom man can and wants to communicate, but the question always remains whether in reality they are not merely natural, impersonal powers that influence man's life.

Another question is whether a certain deity is masculine or feminine. Here, too, we find the same vagueness as between "he" and "it." Numberless peoples have both gods and goddesses. This is partly based on their division of the cosmos. Heaven is masculine, and so are its phenomena. Earth, on the other hand, is feminine; she is the conceiving, parturitional divinity. She is dark and must be cultivated and tilled. Seed must be sown in her. With many peoples these characteristic acts are only performed by women. Woman belongs to the earth; she *is* in a certain sense the earth; she represents the earth. It stands to reason that the divinity of fruitfulness is a goddess. Man originates from her; she is the life-bearing power, is the earth herself: to her man will return when he dies. Entering the grave is as it were re-entering the womb from which man came.

These female deities played a very important part in the various religions. Quite naturally man's relation to her was different from his relation to the father-gods, the male deities. Man's infantile longing for mother, for the safety of mother's embrace, was expressed in the worship of these goddesses. Over against a mother goddess, man's sense of guilt was not as great; he felt himself more one with her. She was his comforter in life's sorrows, his refuge in danger. In Greek mythology Demeter was the mother of grain, the fertile, grain-bearing earth. Her daughter Kore, according to the myth, was abducted by Pluto, the god of the underworld, and taken to his abode. Demeter searched everywhere for her, and while doing so she stopped her work so that the earth no longer bore fruit and the trees lost their leaves. Jupiter decided that Kore should be in the underworld for half a year and the rest of the year in her own world. That is why summer and winter now succeed each other.

It is interesting to note that female deities are not only presented as gentle and helping mothers but that often very terrifying qualities are ascribed to them. Artemis was the Greek goddess of springs and streams, of agriculture and cattle-breeding; but she was at the same time the fearful one who caused death with her dreadful weapons. Hinduism has, besides Lakshmi, the tender goddess of fertility and blessing, Durga or Kali. Durga is the earth, the mother-earth, but she reveals her dangerous attributes: she causes crop failure and trouble. She is represented with a drinking cup in her hand, made from a human skull and filled with steaming blood, and with a chain of skulls around her neck. She is the fearful one, but, indeed, at the same time the mother from which all originates and the terrible destroyer who scatters disaster and distress over the world. Thus the divine mother is at the same time the object of both childlike devotion and also terror.

But who is the deity that bears all and fills all as a hidden power? Is he a male god, a father, as he has been called everywhere by all kinds of peoples at some time or other? Or is it an impersonal power who neither listens to our prayers nor becomes angry at our sins? Or is the deity at the same time both masculine and feminine, both heaven and earth? Mankind has given many answers to these questions, and each answer is always closely connected with a group's attitude to its god. If it considers the deity as the bearer of the universe, an impersonal power, it can let itself sink away in the ocean of his infinity. To find such a god means to be wrapped up in him and to destroy that most difficult thing in man, his "I-sense," his *ahamkara*. For this "I-sense" is the barrier between him and the deity. God can only be met in a state of intoxication or stupefaction.

Another answer is possible when the deity is considered an impersonal power. He can be viewed as *mana*, the supernatural power in objects, in natural phenomena, even in man himself, and man can try to subject and use this power by magic formulas. Here the magician is the one who knows these powers and the way to handle them. But this tendency to dominate this deity, as it were, and make him do man's will, appears also in religions whose adherents bow before a personal god. They may try to coerce the deity by vows, gifts, and diligent service to answer their prayers. We see the ever-returning *do-ut-des* motif — man's attempt to dominate his god in some way or other.

When studying the history of religions it is remarkable how many different ways of communication with the deity we meet. We find both an awful fear of the gods and at the same time an audacious attempt to have power over them. The worshippers flee from the gods, but at the same time they passionately seek and serve them. We find both strict obedience and licentious laxity of morals. We find intoxication and drunkenness alongside scrupulous reckoning with the gods and keeping score of one's good and evil deeds. Mankind has tried every means and every way imaginable. Being part of this mysterious universe in which he finds himself, having some notion of the norm which dominates life and of the riddle that he moves between act and fate, and struggling to be saved, man felt that there must be a divine power higher than himself, and he has ever reached for a vision of it.

CHAPTER VIII

RELIGIOUS CONSCIOUSNESS AND ITS UNCERTAINTIES

When trying to get a general view of the history of religion two things strike us again and again — first, the similarity of the problems with which the different religions have struggled and, second, the great diversity of the answers they have given. First the similarity of the problems, because we find that the five problems which we have enumerated persist. As we have seen, man realized how intimately he was related to the cosmos. He understood that he belonged to it; that he was, as it were, a member of, and a cell in, the great body of the universe. This idea is so fundamental in many religions that nearly all the religious ideas and practices can be explained from it. Man felt that he was an integral part of the natural phenomena; the laws which dominate them dominate his own existence also. To possess religious wisdom meant to behave in harmony with the laws, to fit in with the order of the universe. The division of the tribe, the rules concerning marriage, the order of the religious feasts, were all inspired by the thought that man must be conscious of the fact that he belonged to the cosmic community and that he must subject himself to its rules. The meaning of life was to be harmonically included in the community, and together with it to be included in the totality of heaven and earth.

But as soon as man had accepted this idea, doubt continued to arise. Is man merely an atom in the universe, and nothing more? Does nothing in him transcend the natural order? Is he not at the same time at least an onlooker at the great cosmic play? Does not the fact that he speaks of himself as an "I" prove that he is also something different? Can he disassociate himself to some extent from this cosmos of which he is a member? Or is that *rebellion;* is the word "I" the greatest lie of our existence?

This is the first problem with which man is confronted, a problem which his existence implies and which is in essence religious. Man must solve this fundamental problem, in some way or other. There is no religion which does not struggle to find an answer to these vital questions.

The second problem confronting man concerns the norm. Man ever meets this norm or, rather, the norm meets man. It confronts him in the rules which his parents teach him when he is very young, but somehow its effect implies that its authority exceeds that of the will of his parents. We have seen that primitive religion holds that in prehistoric time the High God or All-father established the morals and rules, which must therefore be respected because they remind us of God. In other religions we see that the norm to which man is subject is in reality only the expression of the cosmic order as applied to human life. A son of one clan of a certain tribe must marry a daughter of another clan of the same tribe, because the one clan represents heaven in the greatest tribalism and the other the earth, and because heaven and earth marry. In the Chinese writing Po Hu T'ung we find the following questions and answers: "Why is it that the Son of Heaven and the Feudal Lords marry nine wives at a time? It is to emphasize the importance of their states and to enlarge their progeny. Why does it happen to be nine? It is modeled after Earth with its nine provinces which, responding to Heaven's creative force, leaves nothing without life."[1] The rules for the emperor and his subjects are patterned after the order of nature.

Nevertheless it did not escape man's observation that the norm contains an element of surprise. True, if man is but an atom in the cosmos, then the all-dominating power of the cosmic order has a hold on him, but this does not mean that he is confronted with a "thou shalt." Even if the very substance of the norm is that man must live in conformity with the structure and the rules of the universe, then the norm implies a certain amount of freedom. This in turn implies that man is able to make a choice, and to do this, he has to be something — something belonging to the cosmos, to be sure, but at the same time something higher, something on a higher plane, as it were. This is the second problem with which every religion struggles, because it is implied in human existence itself.

The third question which every religion faces is the riddle of the life of man. Is life an act, or is it essentially merely fate? We have seen how this problem was approached from different angles by the different religions. Islam approaches it differently from the ancient astral religions of the Near East, and these in turn approach it differently from Hinduism and Buddhism. But there is always a common element; we always have to do with this same puzzle — how man, who knows every moment that he consciously acts, is at times overwhelmed by the queer notion that his life is like a film and that he himself is, as it were, a puppet in the hands of other powers.

When man is considered as merely an atom in the great cosmos, the dilemma is easy to solve. Then it is clear that life is nothing but fate, something that flows over us and in which we do not play an active part. We undergo it, we are carried along by a current; we entertain the illusion that we ourselves are active, but all our activity is only powerless passivity. It is remarkable that some of these religions have

1 Po Hu T'ung, in Tjan Tjoe Som, *The Comprehensive Discussions in The White Tiger Hall.* Leiden: Brill, 1949, p. 251.

actually expressed it this way. But we saw, too, that there was a certain fear to give in to this thought, because that would be denying our own life. Then it would no longer be our life; our acts would no longer be our acts; nothing would be ours, and that short and very mysterious word "I," which we use thousands of times, would become a fatal lie.

In the fourth place we considered the riddle of redemption. Again it is remarkable that the idea of redemption occurs in all religions. Actually there is no religion which accepts existence, as given by nature, as such. Through all these religions runs the notion that something must happen, that a change, that *redemption,* is necessary. Hence man *does* something: children are circumcised, initiated, or admitted into the clan after all kinds of circumscribed ceremonies. But even that is not sufficient. Several religions feel that a more radical redemption is necessary. Hinduism holds that true redemption is only found when man is free from this bewildering world and has become one with Brahman, the origin of all things. In Buddhism redemption has become such a central idea that it concentrates all its attention on it. A cry for redemption resounds through all of the history of religion.

But this fact confronts man once more with the fundamental problem of his existence. Is redemption an act? Can man bring it about himself, or is it merely fate? Does it happen to man, but without his aid? Another equally urgent question is: must man be saved *from* the world, or together *with* it? Is redemption a cosmic thing, or is it something that involves man as an individual? And then the third, inevitable, question is, What is the result of man's redemption? What is this redeemed state for which man longs so passionately? Hence we see that the ideas and expectations regarding redemption multiply.

The fifth riddle which we mentioned is that of the invisible background of all things. The idea that behind this visible world there were mysterious, invisible, supernatural powers was evidently deeply rooted in the heart of man. Often the myths about these powers are very primitive and childlike, but they always contain something of a strange supposition that this world is only one side of reality. There is more to it, and what is hidden is more important and decisive than what is visible. As soon as man tried to penetrate into this mystery, however, he lost his way in a labyrinth of difficulties. Was this invisible something, hidden behind this world, a "he" or a "she" or an "it"? Or was it all three at the same time; or was it a confused community of gods and demons? When man regarded himself as merely a small part of the cosmos, it was only natural for him to think that the gods and demons centered in him, that he was the focus in which all rays met. But were these gods and demons personalities? Did they have a personal will? Or were they merely powers in nature? And did all these mysterious powers merge into one world-soul?

We see that the history of religion depicts a great variety of divine forms and myths. That is why it is such a remarkable history. Again and again the same ideas crop up. Also, this history repeats itself many times. When examining its searching and groping we encounter so many different ideas that we are confused. They are sometimes bizarre, unbelievably child-like and foolish; yet sometimes they strike us as being sublime and imposing. At times these ideas led to inhuman, cruel deeds and dreadful wars, but also to self-denial and neighborly love.

Modern man, nonreligious man included, is confronted with the five questions of which we spoke. For they are basic to his existence and he must respond to them in some way or other. This need not be done philosophically — the answer to these basic problems can be given in the course of everyday life. Everyday actions, one's sense of responsibility or the lack of it, one's ambitions, the things one yearns for, all these are the concrete answer man gives to the basic problems of his existence. That answer is religious — that is to say, it touches the deepest religious realities with which man is confronted. Of course, it may be a negative answer that even denies the existence of invisible backgrounds. But however negative it may be, it responds to the riddles of our existence. Therefore every human life is essentially a choice and a decision. It says something and it does something.

If all this is true, we may ask why these questions, which every religion poses in some way or other, are so unfathomable. I think it is because all these questions concern man's existential relationships. As long as he is occupied with himself only and looks no further, he can fancy himself to be self-sufficient. But as soon as he becomes aware of his relationships, he becomes stupefied, and asks: What am I in this great cosmos? What am I over against the norm, that strange phenomenon in my life that has authority over me? What am I in my life that speeds on and on — a doer or a victim? What am I in the face of that remarkable feeling that overwhelms me sometimes, the feeling that everything must be changed and that things are not right as they are? What am I over against that very mysterious background of existence, the divine powers? It is in this area of existential relations that man is confronted with the crucial matters of life — and one of these is religion. Religion convinces man that there are relations. It reveals the "seams" of creation where one thing is connected with another. We can now give the following definition of religion: Religion is the way in which man experiences the deepest existential relations and gives expression to this experience.

It needs no argument that the five questions which we have discussed up to now, and which all concern the fundamental relations of man, are in essence one. The answer to one of them always implies the answer to the others. We realize, certainly, that we are not dealing with five different relations but who regards either *nirvana,* or money, or *valhalla,* or the well-being of the state, or honor, or being lost in Brahman, as the *summum bonum,* and who, when speaking of redemption, does this in words borrowed from this *summum bonum,* says at the same time what he thinks about the questions concerning the norm, God, and his own place in the cosmos. The one always implies the other. It is impossible to answer partially to the questions regarding existence — every word one speaks touches upon all five questions at the same time. But our investigation has shown that man has often been uncertain. When he started to formulate an answer he dared not follow it through to its logical conclusion because it threatened to throw mankind into precipices which mankind had not suspected. The history of religion reveals a decided hesitation and uncertainty in this respect.

We can say that mankind had to take back its words again and again, and that it never came further than to a partial answer. But even if the answer is partial and uncertain, the fact remains that all questions force themselves upon man as one all-inclusive question: "Who am I, small mortal man, in the midst of all these powerful realities with which I am confronted and with which my life is most intimately related?" This very simple question reveals all the problems of religion in a nutshell.

PART II

IN THE LIGHT OF GOD

CHAPTER IX

HUMAN RELIGION IN GOD'S SIGHT

We have looked at the fascinating subject of human religions and examined the questions they reply to. But we must go further — we must evaluate what we have found. How must we judge these human religions? Are they merely human fantasy or is there something of God in them? Have these pagan peoples — as we call them — truly searched in their own way for God, or is their religion essentially rebellion against God and a flight from God? Once again many questions arise which must be answered.

The first thing we must do now is listen. So far we have simply looked around and reflected, but now it is necessary to listen to what God says. By merely reasoning we cannot obtain a clear view only. God Himself can judge all this human religion correctly. Missionaries from all over the world have become more and more convinced of this since the Conference of Tambaran. We can no longer go by human impressions, and we have learned to begin to listen reverently to God's Word. Hendrik Kraemer, in his books *Christian Message in a Non-Christian World* and *Religion and the Christian Faith,* strongly advocates listening intelligently, and during the last ten years many other authors have followed his example. When listening to God's Word, we want to formulate our findings very briefly. Within the scope of this study it is not possible to deal with all the Bible texts that speak of human religion. We shall therefore confine ourselves to discussing Romans 1, because a further reflection on what is said there will make the points we want to examine clearer to us.

The best way to proceed is to look at the part where Paul speaks of human religion, and examine it verse by verse. Paul is speaking here of the power of the gospel. In verse 17 he says: "For therein is revealed a righteousness of God from faith to faith." Then he goes on in verse 18: "For the wrath of God is revealed from heaven against all ungodliness and unrighteousness of men, who hinder the truth in unrighteousness." The New English Bible has the following: "For we see divine retribution revealed from heaven and falling upon all the godless wickedness of men. In their wickedness they are stifling the truth."

Several thoughts demand our attention. In the first place, it is obvious that Paul wants to say that God evidently deals with man already in this world and that He retaliates for evil. The Apostle returns to this idea several times later on. In the same chapter he says three times over that "God gave them up" (vv. 24, 26, 28), that is to say, God gave them up to the dynamics of their own sinful train of thought. That is the divine retribution which Paul discusses in his epistle.

Our second thought concerns the Apostle's statement concerning hindering the truth. In the Greek language St. Paul uses the word *katechein,* literally, "to keep down." The King James Version translates it by "hold," the New English Bible by "stifle." It seems to me that in this case we should translate it by "repress." We intentionally choose a word which has a specific meaning in psychological literature. Webster's *New Collegiate Dictionary* defines the word "repression" as "the process by which unacceptable desires or impulses are excluded from consciousness and thus being denied direct satisfaction are left to operate in the unconscious." This seems to agree with what Paul says here about human life. But we must mention that the word *repression* has received a wider meaning in more recent psychology. In Freudian psychology it specifically refers to unconscious desires of a more or less sexual nature. In more recent psychology it is also applied to desires and impulses of a very different nature. The impulses or desires which are repressed may be very valuable. Anything that goes contrary to the accepted patterns of life or to the predominant popular ideas may be repressed. Usually this happens unconsciously; a person does not even know that he is doing it; but it does happen and the results can be far-reaching. We are reminded of this psychological phenomenon recently discovered by Paul's usage of this word. He says that man always naturally represses God's truth because it is contrary to his pattern of life. Man's wickedness prevents this truth from reaching him; he automatically represses it.

In verse 19 the Apostle goes on to say: ". . . because that which is known of God is manifest in them: for God manifested it unto them." We must observe that the words "manifest in them" cannot mean that man really sees and understands this. The New English Bible has: "lies plain before their eyes." This seems more correct. Whether man comes indeed as far as seeing it is another matter. It is possible that man does not see it because it is automatically repressed, as a rule.

Verse 20 has an elaboration on the preceding thoughts. It shows that what was summed up in verse 19 as "that which is known of God" can be described as "his everlasting power and divinity." These two words are of great importance. The history of religion shows that man seems to be uncertain as to whether God is a "he" or an "it" — a person or a power. In primitive religions we observe a distinction between animistic tendencies, which regard all supernatural things as persons, and dynamistic tendencies, which regard them as magical powers. Therefore it is very instructive that Paul mentions these two things here — the power and the Godhead. It seems that he immediately wants to preclude every attempt to reduce God to a mere impersonal power; but at the same time he wants to preclude every attempt to make him a "High God," far away in unreachable regions, without any influence on our daily life. Paul says: Through all centuries the fact that God is both a person to whom we can pray and to whom we are responsible, and also everlasting power, forces itself naturally upon man. These two characteristics of God are "clearly seen, being perceived through the things that are made." The New English Bible has: "have been visible to the eye of reason." We prefer the King James Version. The Greek word *nooumena*, literally, "being intelligently observed," does not refer to seeing with the eyes in this case, but neither does it mean that "seeing God's everlasting power and godhead" is attained by a process of reasoning. It is not a logical conclusion, but a flash that comes in a moment of vision. It comes suddenly to man, it overwhelms him. But still it does not lead to knowledge. Man escapes God's grasp, man represses the truth. Therefore he is "without excuse."

Verse 21 repeats that man must in fact be regarded as one who knows: "knowing God, they glorified him not as God, neither gave thanks." In the day of judgment man cannot claim that he did not know God. He knows God, even though he never comes to real knowledge because he is always busy subtly repressing this knowledge. Man desperately clings to his own egocentric pattern of life. As a result man went further and further astray: "all their thinking has ended in futility, and their misguided minds are plunged in darkness." In this connection the Apostle thinks of the pagan religions as he has seen them for himself, with their statues, superstitions, and infatuation. He does not mean to say that these people have consciously or intentionally rejected God's truth. Generally speaking, they do this unconsciously and unintentionally, but they are nevertheless guilty. The aerial of man's heart can no longer receive the wave length of God's voice, even though it surrounds him on all sides. But in his innermost heart man has turned away from God and now God has vanished out of his sight.

The next part shows what is the result of this attitude. It is remarkable that the Apostle uses the verb "exchange" (Greek, *allasso* or *met'allasso*) three times. In doing this he once again touches upon one of those very remarkable phenomena which recent psychology has pointed out. This phenomenon of replacing, of substituting, is so common that we see it everywhere. It has been discovered that these repressed impulses of which we spoke, which "are left to operate in the unconscious," are not dead. They remain strong, and try to reassert themselves again and again. Surely, they play no part in man's conscious life, but they succeed in showing every now and again that they still exist. This has been illustrated by the story of the boy sent out of class at school who kept on throwing stones against the windows of the school to show that he was still there. Freud particularly has called attention to this phenomenon and inaugurated its study. He noticed that the impulses which have been exiled to the unconscious may very well reveal themselves in the errors we make, in our slips of the tongue. But they especially crop up in dreams, for then they get the chance to come to the surface.

This does not mean that they appear openly in dreams. The mind retains a certain censorship which causes them to appear only, or at least preferably, disguisedly. Here the process of exchange or substitution comes into the picture. The repressed impulses do come to the surface, but in a changed form, a substituted form. For example, a person may dream about his father, but when analyzing the dream he realizes that a sexual inclination or relation lies at the bottom of it, something which he would be ashamed to tell his wife. In dreams things have a distorted form; a certain disguise and exchange takes place. Often symbolic figures appear in dreams which point back to what exists in the unconscious. Therefore psychoanalysis attaches much value to dreams, and they are often used to trace the deeper tendencies, the impulses in exile.

It seems to me that Paul touches upon these things. Man has repressed the truth of the everlasting power and the divinity of God. It has been exiled to his unconscious, to the crypts of his existence. That does not mean, however, that it has vanished forever. Still active, it reveals itself again and again. But it cannot become openly conscious; it appears in disguise, and it is exchanged for something different. Thus all kinds of ideas of God are formed; the human mind as the *fabrica idolorum* (Calvin) makes its own ideas of God and its own myths. This is not intentional deceit — it happens without man's knowing it. He cannot get rid of them. So he has religion; he is busy with a god; he serves his god — but he does not see that the god he serves is not God Himself. An exchange has taken place — a perilous exchange. An essential quality of God has been blurred because it did not fit in with the human pattern of life, and the image man has of God is no longer true. Divine revelation indeed lies at the root of it, but man's thoughts and aspirations cannot receive it and adapt themselves to it. In the image man has of God we can recognize the image of man himself.

We have already mentioned that the result was that God gave them up. This is said three times in this short passage. In verse 24 we read that God gave them up to the vileness of their own desires and the consequent degradation of their bodies. In verse 26 this is repeated in the words: "God gave them up unto vile passions." And in verse 28 the Apostle adds that God gave them up unto a reprobate mind. They could no longer resist the powers within which carried them along. Paul no doubt saw in his days abundant proof of this in the degenerated way of life of the Hellenistic world; he saw what man comes to when God gives him up to his desires and passions. He also saw that mythical religion has no weapon against this degeneration. He had learned what happens when man exchanges the true image of God for all kinds of myths. This weakens man's ethical strength because consciously or unconsciously he then forms an idol according to his own liking.

This in summary is what Paul says in this passage regarding natural man's tendencies and inclinations since the beginning of time. The history of religion illustrates this most convincingly. Now there are still a few points which demand our attention.

(1) It is clear that this passage teaches unmistakably that there is a general revelation. Hendrik Kraemer calls the idea "general revelation" a "misleading term."[1] He says: "The whole concept, in its ordinary use, is tainted by all kinds of notions, which are contrary to the way in which the Bible speaks of revelation."[2] This may be true. The cause, no doubt, is that the concept has been used too often in a philosophical sense. Too often it has been taken for granted that man's reason could lead him to develop a certain natural theology. But the revelation of which Paul speaks in this passage is entirely different. He does not have in mind philosophical conclusions of the human mind nor infantile natural theology. The Bible emphasizes God's everlasting concern for man. We read that God "left not himself without a witness" (Acts 14:17). Time and again man knows that God exists and that man is actually confronted with Him; yet each time man suppresses these convictions and flees from them. But God still concerns Himself with man in a very concrete and personal way. We cannot explain how God does this. In Romans Paul speaks about the invisible characteristics of God which He manifests in the things He made. In Acts 14 he mentions the rain and fruitful seasons and the gladness with which He fills our hearts. But much more can be said about this. God has created the first year of man in such a way that during his life as a small child he finds peace and safety only in the protecting and sustaining nearness of his mother, and thus He gives a father and mother something of His own image which they retain in later years. God meets

---

[1] Hendrik Kraemer, *Religion and the Christian Faith*. London: Lutterworth Press, 1956, p. 341.
[2] *Ibid.*, p. 343.

man in storm and thunder as well as in the radiant beauty of a glorious summer morning. God occupies Himself with man's conscience, his innermost being. God reminds him again and again that responsibility and guilt do exist. Who can trace the hidden ways by which God proves His existence to man? God has His own hidden means of approaching man.

If we wish to use the expression "general revelation" we must not do so in the sense that one can logically conclude God's existence from it. This *may* be possible, but it only leads to a philosophical notion of God as the first cause. But that is not the biblical idea of "general revelation." When the Bible speaks of general revelation, it means something quite different. There it has a much more personal nature. It is divine concern for men collectively and individually. God's deity and eternal power are evident; they overwhelm man; they strike him suddenly in moments when he thought they were far away. They creep up on him; they do not let go of him, even though man does his best to escape them. Escaping from them and repressing them is the human answer to God's revelation, an answer that becomes evident in the history of the religion of man.

(2) This explains the existence of phenomenon-religion. The man who believes in gods and spirits and bows before his idols shows that he is touched by God and that God is seeking him. But he shows at the same time that he himself is busy suppressing that which is absolutely necessary for a person to come to God. His image of God is distorted; something essential to it is eliminated from it. He does not do this intentionally, but, all the same, he is without excuse. He received his image of God from his parents; he grew up with the religion to which he adheres. That may be true, of course, but his religious life contains also something very personal, something belonging only to him — while seeking God earnestly he at the same time tries to escape from Him. His religion is always ambiguous, full of hesitation and discrepancies. In the first chapter

we stated that religion, by its very nature, is a response. It is never man seeking and speaking spontaneously; it is always an answer on his part to something that he feels as a revelation. We must now add that all the great religions in history are man's answer embodying this mysterious process of repression.

We can show this concretely. In the night of the *bodhi,* when Buddha received his great, new insight concerning the world and life, God was touching him and struggling with him. God revealed Himself in that moment. Buddha responded to this revelation, and his answer to this day reveals God's hand and the result of human repression. In the "night of power" of which the ninety-seventh sura of the Koran speaks, the night when "the angels descended" and the Koran descended from Allah's throne, God dealt with Mohammed and touched him. God wrestled with him in that night, and God's hand is still noticeable in the answer of the prophet, but it is also the result of human repression. The great moments in the history of religion are the moments when God wrestled with man in a very particular way.

The history of religion contains a dramatic element. It includes the divine approach and human rejection. This rejection is hidden because man apparently is seeking God and serving Him, but the God he seeks is different from the true God because of the uncanny process of repression and exchange that enters in. It seems to me that we can thus formulate the testimony of the Bible concerning human religions.

(3) If this is true, it seems to me that we can make certain distinctions. We can say that natural man is ever busy repressing or exchanging. But does he always succeed to the same degree? That depends on the strength with which God approaches him. God can at times, as it were, stop the noiseless engines of repression and exchange and overwhelm man to such an extent that he is powerless for the moment. There is, also, always the silent activity of the Holy Spirit inside man, even if he resists Him constantly. The way in which Isaiah

speaks of Cyrus, the anointed one, who was called by His name and girded by God (Is. 45:4, 5), indicates that the Bible certainly leaves the possibility open for God to anoint those who do not know Him with His Spirit and to gird them for certain tasks to which He calls them.

This shows that there are gradations in the history of religion. We always encounter the powers of repression and exchange, but that does not mean that they were always of the same nature and strength. We meet figures in the history of the non-Christian religions of whom we feel that God wrestled with them in a very particular way. We still notice traces of that process of suppression and substitution in the way they responded, but occasionally we observe a far greater influence of God there than in many other human religions. The history of religion is not always and everywhere the same; it does not present a monotonous picture of only folly and degeneration. There are culminating points in it, not because certain human beings are much better than others, but because every now and then divine compassion interferes, compassion which keeps man from suppressing and substituting the truth completely.

(4) A final remark we must make in this connection is that this is very important for the fulfillment of the missionary task. When a missionary or some other person comes into contact with a non-Christian and speaks to him about the gospel, he can be sure that God has concerned Himself with this person long before. That person had dealings more than once with God before God touched him, and he himself experienced the two fatal reactions — suppression and substitution. Now he hears the gospel for the first time. As I have said elsewhere, "We do not open the discussion, but we need only make it clear that the God who has revealed His eternal power and Godhead to them, now addresses them in a new way, through our words."[3] The encounter between God and that man enters

---

[3] J. H. Bavinck, *The Impact of Christianity on the Non-Christian World*. Grand Rapids: Eerdmans, 1948, p. 109.

a new period. It becomes more dangerous but also more hopeful. Christ now appears in a new form to him. He was, of course, already present in this man's seeking; and, because He did not leave Himself without a witness, Christ was wrestling to gain him, although he did not know it. John describes this in a most delicate way: the *Logos* "lighteth every man" and "the light shineth in the darkness; and the darkness comprehended it not" (John 1:9, 5). In the preaching of the gospel Christ once again appears to man, but much more concretely and in audible form. He awakes man from his long, disastrous dream. At last suppression and substitution cease — but this is possible only in a faithful surrender.

CHAPTER X

THE BIBLE IS DIFFERENT

When someone of another religion comes into contact with Christianity for the first time, many things strike him. We can imagine that on first sight he finds that the biblical teachings rather resemble those of his own religion. Many such people who read the book of Genesis or the Gospel of John conclude that although there are many differences, the main points resemble their own religious teachings. The Gospel of John mentions "living water" and speaks of the most important questions of human life in a mysterious, mystical way. The image of Jesus as described in this gospel is in many respects typically Eastern and recalls ideas found in India and other countries as well.

Only after penetrating deeper into the range of ideas found in the Bible does it strike such people that the whole atmosphere is different. It is difficult to say which points first make this impression. Maybe they notice that human life and history are taken more seriously than in most other religions. Jawaharlal Nehru once complained that his people used to be characterized by a "lack of historical sense."[1] The histories of many peoples

1 Nehru, *The Discovery of India,* p. 77.

are a mixture of "fact and fiction" — every description of actual happenings is amplified and elucidated by mythic fantasies. The Bible ascribes a much greater relevance to historical events. That is certainly one of the reasons why such a great part of the Bible consists of historical books. It contains many stories of what men have done and of how God has acted. But, not only those historical writings but also the so-called prophetic books attach great value to history. This fact makes the Bible completely different from all other holy books of mankind. When we try to account for the backgrounds of these discrepancies we encounter a few facts which dominate the whole picture right from the very beginning. It is worthwhile to reflect on them.

(1) According to the Bible the world in which we now live is an absolutely abnormal world. Our aeon is a misty, nebulous age in which things are not what they are in reality. One of the consequences of this is that it often seems as if God is absent. God hides Himself: "Verily thou art a God that hidest thyself," Isaiah says (Is. 45:15). It is moving to read the many complaints in the Bible about the secrecy of God. Again and again we read that He hides His countenance, that He does not stretch out His arm, that He does not show His helping hand. Even in the very heart of the gospel we find the touching cry: "Why hast thou forsaken me?"

It is therefore impossible to draw direct conclusions regarding God from this world and human life. The friends of Job, mistaken regarding the cause of Job's sorrow, construct a theology in which Job is accused of all kinds of secret sins. But God is different; one cannot simply draw from the events conclusions with regard to His will. In the universe there are very mysterious powers, uncanny powers which seemingly dominate the world at times, when God hides His countenance and does not stretch out His hand. In the Old Testament we meet again and again the cry for God's intervention: "Oh that thou wouldest rend the heavens, that thou wouldest come down, that the mountains might quake at thy presence!" (Is. 64:1). Nature, too, is obscure. The Psalmist says: "The heavens declare the glory of God; And the firmament showeth·his handi-work" (Ps. 19:1), but elsewhere he mentions Rahab, the symbol of impetuous chaos, monster of primeval time, who is broken in pieces by God (Ps. 89:10) but who nevertheless reveals His power (Ps. 98:3). People pray fervently that God may "awake" and "put on strength," as in the ancient days, in the generations of old (Is. 51:9). We live in a strange world. When Jesus is surprised by a storm, He rebukes the wind (Matt. 8:26) because they and the sea are moved by hostile powers. Nature, which can delight men by her beauty, contains very dark secrets as well.

Other religions have also observed that the world in which we live has contrary aspects. Therefore the thought arose that the god who sustains everything is ambivalent. He has both heavenly aspects and earthly aspects; he is both the creator of all things but at the same time the destroyer; he is worthy to be sought and loved and at the same time whimsical, dreadful, all-devouring. The universe, according to some of these religions, exists by the grace of the cosmic balance, the balance between these creative and destroying powers. Thus man tried to deduce from the cosmos the nature of God and His image.

This very thing the Bible condemns, for it is not possible. One can hear God's voice in nature; everything speaks of Him; but one cannot deduce His image from this whimsical, abnormal world. To be sure, this world is His creation, but in some mysterious way there rests a curse upon it. God is not identical with the world. He absolutely transcends it. He is different from what natural man imagines when he looks about this world.

(2) This biblical revelation about God is based on the idea of the Kingdom of Heaven. This Kingdom must have existed in the beginning, when God created all things and "saw every-

thing that he had made, and, behold, it was very good" (Gen.
1:31). But after that something happened that changed everything. Sin entered in the cosmic palace; laceration and curse
penetrated into the utmost corners of the world. The Bible depicts a most intimate relation between the degeneration of
morals and the cosmic confusion. When in Psalm 82 we read
the complaint that the judges no longer administer justice, the
words "all the foundations of the earth are shaken" follow
at once. The universe shakes on its foundations when moral
order is trampled down in the world of men.

When the Bible uses the expression "Kingdom of God,"
both ethics and the cosmos are included. In that Kingdom
everything will be restored to its right place and order will be
restored in every respect. The mist will lift, the power of the
chaos and the resistance, the "prince of this world" (John 12:
31), will be cast out. This implies that God will once more
ascend His throne and take all life in His hands. This Kingdom
means harmony, complete beauty, and glory. The Bible preferably uses the rich and significant word "peace," *shalom,* for
this concept. This word includes all that is good and valuable.
In the Kingdom sin will have vanished; the curse will be removed. Men shall no longer lay snares for each other; "they
shall beat their swords into plowshares, and their spears into
pruning-hooks" (Is. 2:4). But in nature, too, all will change:
"the wolf shall dwell with the lamb" (Is. 11:6). The ethical and
cosmic order are most intimately related. When the one is
broken, the other breaks as well; when the one comes into
its own again, the other does as well.

(3) In this connection, the moral order must be strongly
emphasized. It is not merely a necessary social arrangement to
prevent society from disintegration. It is much more than
varnashramadharma, rules for the relationships between the
castes. Its roots reach back to God. It is very remarkable that
the Bible links moral order directly with God Himself: "Ye
therefore shall be perfect, as your heavenly Father is perfect"

(Matt. 5:48). Man is made after God's image and in His likeness, and God demands this image back; man must become "man" again in the full and true sense of the word as God had meant it. Hence mankind cannot ignore the moral order. No people are beyond its reach, there are no particular times when the moral norm no longer counts. Of course there exists an endless variety as to the application of the norm to the various relations of social life, but the deepest norm of life itself is unchangeable. This norm is indicated in the Bible every time by the word "love." "Thou shalt love the Lord thy God with all they heart, and with all thy soul and with all thy mind. . . . Thou shalt love thy neighbour as thyself" (Matt. 22:37, 39). John expresses it thus: "God is love; and he that abideth in love abideth in God, and God abideth in him" (I John 4:16). This also means that the moral conduct of man implies a very direct and personal relation to God. It is sometimes expressed that man must "walk before God" (Gen. 17:1), he must be conscious of his relation to God every moment of his life. A man's moral attitude implies a hidden religious relation to God; man is ever doing something with God. And because this is so, we meet with the concepts of grace, remission of sins, etc. in the Bible; indeed, they are the heart of the biblical message. Communion with God is based on the certainty of His grace, and only this certainty gives joy and life.

(4) Against this background history takes on an entirely new aspect. Most peoples considered history as a circular event — the same things repeat themselves endlessly. In the Bible, history is seen as a dramatic encounter between man and God. History is never enacted merely on a horizontal plane; there is always a vertical dimension also. This is clear from the fact that man, both individually and collectively, must constantly determine his attitude to God, and consequently lives according to this attitude. But it is also clear from the fact that God continually concerns Himself with man and speaks to him.

God has a plan for the world. That is the meaning of history. He sometimes lets the nations walk in their own ways (Acts 14:16), but that does not mean that He is not deeply interested in what they do. The Old Testament emphasizes time and again that Israel lived among other peoples as a powerful witness of God. In what happened with Israel, in its glory as well as in its humiliation, the nations round about could see, if they took the trouble, the majesty and justice of God. Through Israel God was dealing with those nations. It is very remarkable to what extent Israel itself was conscious of this. Particularly in critical moments the Israelites were concerned about what the peoples round about them would think of Israel's God. The honor of God was continually at stake. In the Old Testament we sometimes get the impression that God *played* with the history of the world. When Israel was unfaithful and forsook God, He sent foreign powers, Assyria and Babylon, to oppress His people so that they were nearly annihilated; and only a small part was saved. Afterwards God sent Cyrus, the king of the Persians, to free Israel, and God called him "His anointed" (Is. 45:1).

God often remains hidden so that one would think He does not exist, but He executes His plans in spite of the manifold events of history. Even though it seems at times as if things take their own course, God has a hand in them more than we think. Even in this misty age, He is far more actually King than we suppose, although we can see practically nothing of His Kingdom.

God guides the history of this world toward the inauguration of His Kingdom. Everything, in fact, will terminate in it. The Bible is essentially eschatological, even in the Old Testament. Israel used to look backwards to the great moments of its history. In the first place we can mention the exodus out of Egypt. God was on that occasion their great Savior in a very direct and concrete sense. In the miracles described in the book of Exodus, He, the hidden God, proved His presence in a visible way. Therefore the people of Israel remembered the wonderful days of the exodus during the dark periods of their history and yearned that God would prove His presence in the same way once more. The second great period on which Israel liked to look back was that of the reign of David and Solomon, when it seemed that the fullness of time had arrived and the Kingdom of God would appear gloriously. The great disappointment that followed left an ineffaceable mark on the character of Israel's religious life.

In the New Testament things are wholly different. The secret of the Kingdom unfolded itself in a way that can only astonish us. With the appearance of Jesus Christ the Kingdom arrived; slowly it dawned on man that this aeon of mist and haze could not end until the great event took place which is called in the Bible "reconciliation." This world could not simply drift into the Kingdom of salvation. Man was surrounded by tensions he could not fathom; there existed something called the wrath of God that concerned the confusion man brought about. There was something called demonic domination which held man in its grip from age to age and from day to day. Something had to be fulfilled of which nobody then had any notion, which still remains a great mystery even though we know it now. In Christ the all-pervasive act of salvation came about. His cross and His resurrection are the heart of the history of the world. When Peter speaks of these things, he says that "angels desire to look into" them (I Pet. 1:12). The New Testament shows clearly that Jesus' disciples at first did not have the slightest idea of what took place before their very eyes. They considered the suffering and death of Jesus simply a fearful injustice and at the end of all certainty. Only when everything was past, the Holy Spirit carefully made it clear to them what Christ had done for the world. Only then they began to understand that the events of the Old Testament, that is to say, the two glorious periods of the exodus and the reign of David, had been small signs of the great work of Jesus Christ. The morning of the resurrection, Easter morning, was the beginning of the new aeon; the bells of a new age began to peal, and the Kingdom of God was ushered in.

This is not the place to go further into these things. Theologians have reflected on them from the first century on, and have tried to make it somewhat understandable to our human minds, but they have always ended by the humble admission that we are confronted by things whose existence we realize respectfully and gratefully, but at the same time we admit that they surpass our understanding. Man must find out for himself how strange and obscure our world is; he must feel something like homesickness for the Kingdom in which God will be all and in all, if he is to know what the work of Jesus Christ was and is. Therefore it can be said that the message of the Bible is concentrated in Him. He says of Himself that He is the "way, and the truth, and the life" (John 14:6). He is not only the bearer of the message concerning the Kingdom, but He is also the substance of this message. He is a prophet in a very different sense from that of any other prophet. Christ is the center of Christianity, but in a way that is very different from the ways in which Buddha and Mohammed are centers of their religions.

(5) The New Testament frequently states that a new aeon began on the day of the resurrection of Christ. We are now in the last hour before the red morning sky of the new Day, the Day of the Lord, as the Old Testament likes to call it. It is undeniable that Paul, and the early Christian Church as well, expected the end of the world and the coming of the Kingdom soon. It appears that they were mistaken. God's plan with the history of the world was greater and more majestic than they could then suppose. Jesus pointed out that "this gospel of the kingdom shall be preached in the whole world for a testimony unto all the nations; and then shall the end come" (Matt. 24:14). The first disciples had no idea what this meant. Their world was much smaller than ours. God's plan contained the development of technics that would cause, as it were, the shrivelling up of our globe that would result

in a greater contact between the continents — that bewildering development of which we are witnesses. But the world is still enveloped in mist. The new aeon is at hand, it is present in Jesus Christ, but it cannot develop fully as yet. God's plan is not fully realized. He still speaks to mankind and in this great dialogue His Church is involved.

At the beginning of this chapter we said that someone of another religion who enters the world of the Christian faith, notices that the atmosphere is different in this new world. Countless words and expressions may be the same, but the whole context is different. Ethics receive a different emphasis; history is considered differently; God Himself stands in the center of life; Jesus Christ is unique and incomparable.

We now come back to the five magnetic questions we discussed earlier. That means that we wish to speak about man as a member of the cosmic community, about the religious norm, about man between act and fate, about the longing for redemption, and after that we will speak of God Himself. We met these five questions in every religion, for they are the canvas on which all religions are embroidered. What is their place in the gospel of Jesus Christ? When we go into this more deeply we can draw clearer lines of demarcation between the gospel and the "messages" of the religions of the world.

CHAPTER XI

MAN AS AN ATOM IN THE COSMIC TOTALITY

It must strike many religious non-Christian people, when they come in contact with the Christian faith, that it says much about man but little about the place of man in the world. The Church emphasizes the necessity of conversion, the necessity of faith in Jesus Christ, the service of God, and many other things, but is almost totally silent on the cosmic universe. Man is considered as an active being who must make his own decisions and who must be reconciled with God. He stands apart; his relationship to the cosmos is hardly mentioned.

Many converts feel this as a deliverance. Other religions exhaust themselves in contemplation on the structure of the cosmos and the cosmic order, which must be reverently observed. The Christian faith sets man apart immediately. It does not go deeply into the structure of the cosmos or into ontological conceptions about God, but it emphasizes God's will. God wants us to believe and to surrender ourselves to Him — that is the most important thing. Kraemer has pointed out that in our contact with other religions we must emphasize biblical realism and "the prophetic voluntaristic conception of the Bible."[1] The average missionary actually does this. He

---

[1] Kraemer, *The Christian Message* . . . , p. 115.

does not discuss the structure of the universe with Hindu philosophers, or the god of heaven and the goddess of the earth with people of primitive religion; he does not debate on *tao* with Chinese thinkers. Instead he awakens people to the necessity of conversion. But it is quite possible that this approach causes disappointment to some. It gives them the feeling that the Bible concentrates its message so much on man and his work and on his redemption that the cosmos as a whole does not receive any attention. They feel that the Christian faith is theocentric and anthropocentric, and that the cosmos is left out completely. The Christian faith is a conversation between God and man, and between man and God.

But there is little reason for this disappointment, at least when we listen to what the Bible has to say about these things. It is not impossible that Western civilization, under all kinds of influences, has degraded nature too much to an object, a thing, in the course of its long history, and has lost sight of man's relationship to nature; but the Bible has not neglected this relationship in any way. On the contrary, it plays a very important part in the totality of the biblical message.

It certainly strikes us that the Bible regards the cosmic community in an entirely different way from those of other religions. But that does not mean that the Bible does not think this community important. This is very clear, particularly in the Old Testament.

In the first place we must mention the creation of man as described in Genesis 1. There we read the words that dominate the whole biblical anthropology: God formed man from the dust of the ground and breathed into his nostrils the breath of life. This is made even clearer by the sentence "and God created man in his own image, in the image of God created he him." Two things stand out clearly. The first is that man belongs to the earth; his name is *Adam,* which means *earth.* He is part of the cosmos, which is *his* cosmos. When he dies, he returns to the dust; he will lose himself in the cosmos. This fact is so important in the Bible that it returns again and again.

Man is *Adam,* one who is connected with the cosmos. It is
remarkable that whereas in the Indo-Germanic languages the
word for "man" seems to point back to the fact that man is
endowed with a spirit and a mind, which distinguishes him
from the animals, in the Bible man is called after the earth,
that is to say, after that aspect of his being that is related to the
earth and to all that lives on the earth. Man is in the first place
a member of the cosmic community; he is *Adam.* That means
that according to the biblical idea his fate is related to that of
the whole world.

But this does not wholly solve the riddle of man. Something
in man transcends his being dust — he is made in God's image
and after God's likeness. It is very difficult to formulate what
exactly is meant by "image" and "likeness," but one thing is
certain — this image and this likeness guarantee the unique
place of man in the world. He can, like Francis of Assisi,
speak of "his sister the sun," but he is always superior to it.
Although a tiny bacterium or a wave of the ocean can destroy
him in one moment, he stands fundamentally above all other
creatures. In Psalm 8 we find a hymn of wholehearted marvel-
ing at the unique place of man in the universe: "Thou hast
made him but a little lower than God (*Elohim*), and crownest
him with glory and honour. Thou makest him to have dominion over the works of thy hands" (vv. 5, 6). The place of man
is depicted here in a few words. He is *Adam,* a cell in the
immense body of the universe; but he is made after God's
likeness; something in him makes him unique and gives him
dominion. Earlier we noted that in many religions of the
world there is the so-called sense of cosmic relationship, the
sense of being a member of the cosmic community. We have
also said that modern civilization fosters a sense of being
elevated on a platform. Biblically speaking, we could say that
man, *Adam,* although bound to the cosmos, is allowed to be
God's delegate in the world in virtue of his special vocation.

We will now pay attention to all the passages in the Bible that
have reference to the cosmic community and to man's place

in it. It strikes us immediately that there is a remarkable analogy between what happens with man and with the cosmos. In this analogy man leads the way — what he does and what happens to him is, as it were, projected on a larger scale and receives cosmic dimensions. But man, who leads the way, must make the pattern of his behavior according to God's activity. The basis of the fourth commandment, that man must keep the sabbath holy, is "for in six days the Lord made heaven and earth" (Ex. 20:10). The rhythm of God's activity is projected into human existence. And because man keeps the sabbath, the rhythm of his life is projected into that of his cattle and his field. Indeed, God demands expressly of Israel that when it has reached the promised land "then shall the land keep a sabbath unto Jehovah. Six years thou shalt sow thy field, but in the seventh year shall be a sabbath of solemn rest for the land" (Lev. 25:2-4). Man must follow the pattern of the divine activity. He must lead the way in the cosmos and impress his pattern on the life of the world.

This analogy between man and cosmos reached a dramatic culmination point in the terrifying moment when man, as a result of his desire to be as God, broke away from the protecting fellowship with God and was on his own (Gen. 3:5). In that moment not only his own fate but also that of the whole cosmos was at stake. The Bible here discusses things that explain the whole life and thought of man through the ages. Although man broke the fellowship with God and hid himself from the presence of the Lord, God Himself restored this fellowship and asked for him. The penetrating question of God: "Where art thou?" still lies at the bottom of all human existence. Wandering man, who lost his certainties and could no longer find any meaning in his existence, is still sought by God. The coming of God to man brought judgment that did not concern just man but in some way the whole cosmos — "cursed is the ground for thy sake" (v. 17). That is the deepest cause of the mist that envelops this aeon. We live in an abnormal world because man himself is no longer normal according to the plan of God. But the cosmic connection with man still obtains. Fallen man now lives in a world that lies under a curse. Nature itself groans under the terror that has come upon it, as Paul expresses it. The created universe was made the victim of frustration, not by its own choice, but because of him who was the cause of it. "Up to the present, we know, the whole created universe groans in all its parts as if in the pangs of childbirth" (Rom. 8:20-22, NEB).

The prophet Jeremiah particularly points out that man himself, in his sinful self-preservation, often disturbs the analogy of nature. In nature, even though it lies under a curse, something of the divine order is still present, but man does not care about this order: "The stork in the heavens knoweth her appointed times; and the turtledove and the swallow and the crane observe the time of their coming: but my people know not the law of Jehovah" (Jer. 8:7). Man, fallen out of step, is the great spoiler of the cosmic unity, and therefore he is the loneliest creature in the cosmic community.

The Bible depicts this loneliness of sinful man in the world in a sometimes striking way. It seems as if nature is disgusted at the baseness of man: "The land is defiled: therefore I do visit the iniquity thereof upon it, and the land vomiteth out her inhabitants" (Lev. 18:25). Man leaves his traces of destruction, of burning forests, of damaged villages and towns in the world. The whole world is carried along by his impulse to destroy. The destroyed land vomits him out, as it were. Jeremiah describes the terror of a country where war has raged in words which almost remind us of what we may have to go through in our atomic age: "I beheld the earth, and, lo, it was waste and void. . . . I beheld the mountains, and, lo, they trembled. . . . I beheld, and, lo, there was no man, and all the birds of the heavens were fled. . . . I beheld, and, lo, the fruitful field was a wilderness" (Jer. 4:23-26). Proud man plays his wild game with God's world, yet God expressly protects nature from man. In His rules of warfare God says: "When thou shalt besiege a city a long time, in making war against it

to take it, thou shalt not destroy the trees thereof by wielding
an axe against them" (Deut. 20:19). The Bible sometimes indicates very carefully that criminal and God-forsaken man
infects nature, as it were. Man's behavior threatens nature itself with the power of his chaos. This thought lies at the root
of God's demand to atone for leprosy and to cleanse all kinds
of objects from sin. Leviticus 14:20 says that the priest must
make atonement for the leper because of his leprosy. The word
"atonement" (Hebrew *kafar,* "cover") has a much wider connotation than simply taking away sin; it means also the re-
moval of things and people from the curse and defilement to
which they are subjected. In other places cleansing and puri-
fication are mentioned. Leviticus 8:15 says that Moses "purified the altar," Leviticus 14:52 that the house where a leper
lived must be cleansed or purified. The same verb, which literally means "to unsin," and is translated by "to purify" or
"cleanse" is also used in Ezekiel's prophecies of the cultic objects (Ezek. 43:22; 45:18). It means that these objects must
be withdrawn from the atmosphere of corruption and defilement
by which everything on earth is affected.

We can hardly imagine how intensely and concretely the
prophets of the Old Testament regarded these things. The
prophet Habakkuk describes how the people of the Chaldeans
built up their kingdom by force. He compares it with a house,
and then says, "Thou hast devised shame to thy house, by cut-
ting off many peoples, and hast sinned against thy soul. For
the stone shall cry out of the wall, and the beam out of the
timber shall answer it" (Hab. 2:10). Even the lifeless objects
are involved in the drama of man and his world.

It needs no argument that these ideas come to expression
in the biblical view of Israel's cult. Countless peoples regard
their temples as a miniature representation of the cosmos. The
temple is the *meru,* or mountain of the gods, around which lies
the flat earth surrounded by the world-ocean. This pattern is
not difficult to point out in numberless sanctuaries all over the

world.[2] There is reason to think that the Temple of Solomon in Jerusalem also represented the cosmos. In this Temple there was not a *meru* rising high above the plain, but deep inside there was the Holy of Holies with the Ark, the permanent sign of God's presence. The Holy of Holies itself was a kind of distant memory of Paradise. Above the Ark there were cherubim, just as Paradise was cut off by cherubim in primeval time. No man was allowed to enter the Holy of Holies except the priest, and that only once a year. The Temple as a whole faced east, to where the sun rises. The carvings in the Temple all reminded the people of the world; there were cherubim and palm trees and open flowers. It seemed as if the whole world was represented in the small space of the Temple.

It would carry us too far if we went into all the details. We point out merely that the colors used in the Temple and the measurements of the parts and the place of each part had their own special meaning. They were symbols of things which in a few instances we can sense but which in other cases are completely obscure. Nothing was merely neutral; numbers and colors, in short, all particulars, were signs through which God had something to say. In them God wrote His holy will and plan for the world.

This is undoubtedly the reason for the exact description given in the Bible and for the emphasis that everything must be made exactly in accordance with God's instruction. No deviation was allowed, because everything constituted a significant whole. We may be surprised that the admonition "that he die not" (Ex. 28:33-35) is added to the simple command to sew bells of gold on the robe of Aaron before entering the Temple as a high priest. But in the total context of Israel's cult these things were far more important than we are apt to think. Every detail was meant to make clear God's intention.

This does not mean, however, that these colors, objects, and numbers were meant to have a sort of magical effect, as in all

2 Heine-Geldern, *Weltbild und Bauform in Süd-Ostasien.*

the other religions, where it is thought that particular colors, objects, numbers, days, hours, and natural phenomena indeed have a magical power. These people, who believe that such things can cause evil or good, also believe that they can manipulate them to certain ends. But in the Bible we find nothing of the kind. There things always remain *things;* they never have a supernatural power. Even the holiest object in the cult, the so-called Ark of the Testimony, appeared to be powerless, so that at one time the enemy captured it when the Israelites took it to the battlefield to insure the victory. In the Bible things are only things, but they have a meaning; they are letters in God's speech, they are words in which He expresses His thought and thus their symbolic value far exceeds their intrinsic value. The intimate relation between man and the cosmos is most obvious in the places where the Bible speaks of redemption in the future. This redemption never concerns man alone, but always man and his world, which can never be separated. We have quoted the words of Paul, "the whole created universe groans in all its parts." In the same context he says that "there was always hope, because the universe itself is to be freed from the shackles of mortality and enter upon the liberty and splendor of the children of God" (Rom. 8:21). When in autumn a storm rages and all of nature groans, then man sees before his eyes something of this truth. The Old Testament often expresses the same thought in even more concrete language. Isaiah says, in moving language: "The wolf shall dwell with the lamb, and the leopard shall lie down with the kid. . . . They shall not hurt nor destroy in all my holy mountain; for the earth shall be full of the knowledge of Jehovah, as the waters cover the sea" (Is. 11:6, 9). This is what we have called the great peace, the *shalom,* the chief feature of the Kingdom of God. All creatures share in this *shalom.* Of course, man is very much the main concern. In chapter 25 Isaiah speaks about the feast the Lord of hosts will make unto all people: "And He will destroy . . . the face of the covering that covereth all peoples, and the veil that is spread over all nations" (v. 6).

In his mind he sees the nations of the whole world coming to the feast of God, when "they shall beat their swords into plowshares" (2:4). The prophet depicts this wonderful future very dramatically for an agricultural nation such as Israel: "And it shall come to pass in that day, I will answer, saith Jehovah, I will answer the heavens, and they shall answer the earth; and the earth shall answer the grain, and the new wine, and the oil; and they shall answer Jezreel" (Hos. 2:21). The various realms in the cosmos begin to listen to each other again and to fulfill each other's wishes. A new harmony comes about, and all of creation is at peace. Every time the Old Testament speaks of the future, of the great Day of the Lord, it first mentions dreadful things that will take place in the world of mankind, but then it focuses its attention on the new humanity and the new world. The redemption of man concerns all of nature. Right to the end man is in close connection with nature. They were one in creation; they were and are one in humiliation and curse; they will be one in redemption.

The New Testament develops these thoughts further. In the gospels we read about the miracles Jesus did as signs of the Kingdom of Heaven. These miracles were not performed to astonish men, although this was often the consequence. By these miracles Jesus wanted to make clear that the whole cosmos will be redeemed, and that the curse which threatened the life of man through all the ages will be withdrawn. So He opened the eyes of the blind, made the lame to walk, and even raised the dead. All these miracles were signs that in Him the Kingdom of God was at hand. A new aeon had dawned, a new age, not only for man but for the whole universe. Jesus Himself speaks of the coming regeneration as having cosmic dimensions (Matt. 19:28). His resurrection from the dead is the first sign of this regeneration; that is why Christ's resurrection is the heart of the New Testament message. Paul has elaborated on these things, especially in one of the most difficult parts of one of his letters, Ephesians 1. He says: "God has made known unto us the mystery of his will, according to his good pleasure which he purposed in him unto a dispensation of the fulness of the times, to sum up all things in Christ, the things in the heavens, and the things on the earth" (vv. 9-10). The words "to sum up" contain the tragedy of the world as it is now. The world in which we now live is divided; its different parts are out of harmony. Man is a stranger in nature; his moral capabilities do not match his technical power, and the latter is a threat to himself. Everything is disrupted, and peace and harmony are violated everywhere. But God is going to gather together all things in Christ, and is already doing it in preparation for the fullness of the times. The bringing of the message of Christ all over the world unites people of different races and civilizations around one Holy Communion table. At times we see the beginning of the realization of the "gathering together" which expresses God's intention concerning the world. But that is only the beginning, for God wants to go further. His ultimate intention is described in the last book of the Bible: "And I saw no temple therein: for the Lord God the Almighty, and the Lamb, are the temple thereof" (Rev. 21:22).

In our time we still struggle with the idea of the Kingdom of God. For a long time Christians have overemphasized the fact that the Christian faith is something that concerns man's innermost being and is the way to salvation, without paying enough attention to the fact that faith places man in the perspective of the Kingdom. That includes the fact that the believer must strive after a new world. Something of the power of the new life in Jesus Christ must penetrate social and economic life, commerce and industry, science and art. We must not leave any sector of individual or social life to its own devices. God wants us to gather together right now all things in this world under one head, Christ. It goes without saying that this matter is very much of current interest in our modern world. Modern life is too compartmentalized. The university has too little to do with the church, the church in turn too little with the factory. Political and economic powers develop according to their inherent dynamics. One of the reasons why first national-socialism and then communism fascinated and still fascinate so many people is that both vigorously tried, and still try, to "gather all things together." In both systems the university is allowed to teach only what the Party commands, the newspapers can publish only what the Party prescribes, art must create only what flatters the Party. Such uniformity can, of course, only be achieved by force. Great concentration camps are necessary to realize this ideal. Democracy, on the other hand, must run the risk of the various powers growing away from each other and of chaos developing where the necessary harmony is completely absent. In our modern world we reach for social forms that create peace and harmony. No word is more fascinating to us than the biblical word "peace," *shalom,* in its radical biblical sense. But this *shalom* cannot be created by concentration camps and coercive measures. All such attempts are bound to fail because God does not allow man to steal his plan from Him. God is actively engaged preparing this *shalom* through Christ, in whom He extended His hand to this confused world.

Therefore it is worth noticing how, from the point of view of faith in Jesus Christ, even ordinary things become different and receive an orderly relation. In this connection I think of numbers in arithmetic. They are of great importance to the human mind and in human life, perhaps of greater importance than they deserve. Nevertheless God reveals something of His intentions with these numbers and their relations. The simple fact that one and one is two and that one minus one is zero shows in arithmetical form the majesty of God's justice. A thing that belongs to me I can give away only once. I can pass through every day of my life only once because one minus one is nought. I increase my guilt and responsibility when I go on with my mistakes, because one and one is two. In this simple arithmetical order we see how unavoidable and serious life is. That must be what struck the poet of Psalm 90 when he said, "For all our days are passed away in thy wrath. . . . So teach us to number our days, That we may get us a heart of wisdom" (vv. 9, 12). Arithmetic has something to do with God's justice.

On the other hand, arithmetic brings us into contact with God's miracles. For God breaks the arithmetical order time and again. Biology confronts us with this miracle. Jesus Himself points out (in the well-known parable) that seeds multiply so that they bring forth fruit, some an hundredfold, some sixtyfold, some thirtyfold (Matt. 13:8). In living nature a number is a totally different power from what it is in inorganic matter. Two people can "become one flesh," and consequently they can become entire nations. By His power God breaks the order we have learned in our books. Mankind exists only by the grace of this miracle, for because of it man's granaries are filled and there is daily food for him. The order of numbers also tells us something of God's care for mankind.

As soon as it comes to psychology, I notice that numbers do not exist there. I cannot say that I like one friend twice as much as another, or that I am three times as happy today as I was yesterday. Every quantitative difference in psychology becomes suddenly a qualitative difference. Everything that is larger or more intense is suddenly different. Realizing this, our eyes are opened to the relativity of numbers. There are, thank God, things that cannot be weighed or measured; there are situations where numbers are out of place, situations that are greater and more life-forming than arithmetic.

Finally, numbers get a new meaning in theology. It is remarkable that in the Bible God always resists human arithmetic. When in the days of the prophet Malachi the people of Israel refused to give their tithes for the Temple service, they did so because of their reasoning that ten minus one is nine. But the prophet repudiated this. He said in the name of the Lord: "Bring ye the whole tithe into the store-house, that there may be food in my house, and prove me now herewith, saith Jehovah of hosts, if I will not open you the windows of heaven, and pour you out a blessing, that there shall not be room enough to receive it" (3:10). In other words, ten minus one is much more than nine when I faithfully take God's presence into account. When the disciples thought that a few loaves of bread were not enough to feed a great multitude, Jesus reproved them and showed them how a number becomes a completely different power when He handles it.

These considerations teach us that the Bible has more to do with our arithmetic book, and has more authority over it, than we think. The Bible makes the ordinary, everyday things including our arithmetical order, transparent to us. It reveals its depth and teaches us that God's presence is expressed in this simple order. It gathers together the various branches of our knowledge and work and places these different fields under one head, Christ. This is the wonderful idea of the Kingdom. God gathers together, and He is doing it right now, in *this* world. He wants us to do it too, in Him.

CONCLUSION

When we consider all these things we must come to the conclusion that the Bible teaches that in God's sight man is in the heart of the cosmos. As God's delegate he is directly connected with God and yet closely connected with the whole world. He is in the cosmos; he is part of it; but in a special way, because he is made after the image of God, a little lower than God (Ps. 8). Therefore he is a leader in the world and exercises dominion. It is his world; and together with it he is God's property, God's creature. In many respects he sets the tone in the world — his conduct can destroy the cosmos or be a blessing to it. Together with the world he bears the curse, together with the world he is saved. Thus we may describe the biblical view of man as a member of the cosmic community.

It would be going too far to examine how the idea of man's place in the cosmos originated in the Christian Church. People have often tried to express this in the Church's liturgy as well as in its architecture. Churches were built facing the east. The gospel was read from a desk at the north side. Every facet of the liturgy was given its own place as based on the structure of the cosmos. Many of these things have fallen into disuse during the centuries and are now no longer noticed, but the forms in which they are expressed are not the important thing. The essential thing is that the Church is conscious of the place of man in the cosmos and of the great prospect of the "gathering together" in the Kingdom of God.

CHAPTER XII

THE LAW OF THE KINGDOM

In the message of the Bible, the concept *law* occupies an important place. In the Old Testament it sometimes seems to be so important that it overshadows everything else. But on second sight it appears that the law, although it is very important, is always to be seen against the background of two other concepts, the Kingdom and merciful redemption. The redemptive interest is clearly seen in the law of the Ten Commandments. It begins with the words, "I am the Lord, thy God, who brought thee out of the land of Egypt, out of the house of bondage: thou shalt have no other gods before me." The commandment is based on the relation of the covenant. Paraphrased, it says, "I am thy God; I have delivered thee out of Egypt; I have made of thee a people, a free and independent people — thou shalt have no other gods before me." The strongly spiritual and moral motive of the law is the merciful relationship and the deliverance from the "house of bondage."

In the second place, the law is always somehow connected with the idea of the Kingdom. This connection especially deserves our attention. We know that every faithful Israelite considers Jahweh King of this world. The Israelite knows, as we mentioned before, that it sometimes seems that all kinds of other powers have taken control of the world. God often seems absent; His omnipotence is sometimes obscured. In Psalm 44:23-24 the poet cries out to God, "Awake, why sleepest thou, O Lord? . . . Wherefore hidest thou thy face?" In this scheme of things we meet a God who is apparently sleeping while the powers of chaos sweep over the world. The latter may be the case at times, but every pious Israelite is nevertheless strongly convinced that God is King. In Psalm 22: 28 this is emphatically stated: "For the kingdom is Jehovah's, And he is the ruler over the nations." "Jehovah reigneth; let the peoples tremble: He sitteth above the cherubim; let the earth be moved" (Ps. 99:1). The people realized that the shining throne of the Lord is not visible for them: "clouds and darkness are round about him: Righteousness and justice are the foundations of his throne" (Ps. 97:2). When King Solomon built the Temple in Jerusalem, he expressed this idea in the Temple's architecture — the Holy of Holies, the place where Jahweh's throne stood among the cherubim, was completely dark. Solomon stated: "Jehovah hath said that he would dwell in the thick darkness" (I Kings 8:12). The word *darkness* used here means especially the darkness resulting from dark clouds and dark mist. The throne of Jehovah is surrounded by a dark fog. No man can verify His policy. Every day we are confronted with the great mysteries of His divine government. Right up to Golgotha the anxious question "Why" sounded. Nevertheless, God is King and His Kingdom is an everlasting Kingdom (Ps. 145:13). It is quite clear that the idea of the Kingdom is very closely connected with that of the law or the norm — the Kingdom is held together by the law. Therefore the law has a universal character and concerns all creatures. This thought is strikingly apparent in the description of the ordinances we find in the Old Testament. The Hebrew language uses the noun *hok* or *hukah* or the verb *hakak* in that case. The remarkable thing is that these three words are applied not only to the human world and the divine ordinances concerning human life, but also to nature. In nature, too, these ordinances are engraved, as it were.

The prophet Jeremiah, who (as we have already seen) contemplates on the whole of nature, wants to show that God has also made laws for nature. In chapter 31, verses 35 and 36, speaking of the command to the moon and to the stars to be a light by night, he says, "If those ordinances depart from me, saith the Lord, then the seed of Israel also shall cease from being a nation before me for ever." In Jeremiah 33:25 the prophet applies the concept "covenant" (*berith*) to the relation between God and nature: "Thus saith the Lord; if my covenant be not with day and night, and if I have not appointed the ordinances of heaven and earth. . . ." The ordinances which God has inscribed in nature result from the covenant that He has made with this whole cosmos.

In other parts of the Old Testament the meaning of these ordinances is further unfolded. In Job 38, different constellations are mentioned — the Pleiades, Orion, the Zodiac; and then the question is put: "Knowest thou the ordinances of heaven? Canst thou set the dominion thereof [namely of heaven] in the earth?" (vv. 31-33). This is a very concrete example of the influence of the celestial powers on earthly life. The appearance of particular constellations in the nocturnal sky was a sign to the farmers that the time was come to sow or to do other things. The sky shows what must happen on earth, for God has written these ordinances in the stars.

A totally different aspect of the ordinances is elucidated in Psalm 148 and Proverbs 8. In Psalm 148:6 the poet speaks of the heaven and of the waters that are above the heavens. He says that God established them for ever and ever: "he hath made a decree which shall not be transgressed." The same thought is found in Proverbs 8:22: "The Lord possessed me [wisdom] in the beginning of his way, before his works of old." In verse 27 the teacher goes on to say that "When he prepared the heaven, I was there: when he set a compass upon the face of the depth [the *tehom*]." In verse 29 the argumentation is continued: "When he gave to the sea his decree, that the waters should not pass his commandment: when he appointed the foundations of the earth." In this part the words *hok* and *hakak* occur several times. The sense of these texts is undoubtedly that God, when ordering this creation, put everything in its right place and appointed its boundaries. Nothing must become stronger and go beyond its boundaries. The sea must not pass her bounds contrary to God's will; creatures are not allowed to extend their domain, or to annex power and place to themselves which are not theirs. These ordinances which God has inscribed in this world shall not be transgressed. This last statement is remarkable, for it seems as if the ordinances that God has imposed on nature leave room for the possibility that nature may be disobedient. In comparison, the natural phenomena are given an independent power of decision to obey or not, with the fortunate result that they all accede to God's government. Then we recall Jeremiah's assertion that man alone is different. Man is the lonely transgressor in the cosmos; he has deserted his place. But the tragedy of his existence is that he involves nature in his degeneration. He himself again becomes a prey to the powers of the chaos, and involves nature in this chaos as well.

These different thoughts make the meaning of the norm clear. The norm demands that everything remain in its own place and not interfere with God's order. Every point on a circle is determined by its relation to the other points on the circle and also by its relation to the center of the circle; this could be an example of what the norm actually is. The divine law, or the ordinances, in essence are meant to safeguard the world in its living relationship to God. This means that everything, each constellation, each plant, each animal, each man, each atom, must be in the place where God has put it, and must not make itself larger than it is. It must not try to be like God and place itself in the center. As soon as it does this, the relationship to God is broken, and with it the cosmic relationship. Existing always includes two things: it means standing before God, being in relationship to Him, and it means being a living member in the great relationship of creation, in the Kingdom of God. Therefore the norm says to every creature: be in accordance with God's intention! Beware of going beyond the boundaries! If we were to ask the question whether the Bible knows the conception "cosmic order" as the Vedas know the *rta* and the Chinese the *tao,* we can in a certain sense answer affirmatively. But in the Bible this order has never been substantiated, never been made an independent power. It never comes between us and God, as a power on its own. There is a cosmic order, there are ordinances which apply to man and all other creatures, but these ordinances exist only through God. They express God's will. In these ordinances every creature is involved with God.

When it comes to a further elaboration of this cosmic order, the Bible emphasizes two fundamental relations, the relation of man to God and to his neighbor. These two are stipulated in the great commandment: "Thou shalt love the Lord thy God with all thy heart, and with all thy soul, and with all thy mind. This is the first and great commandment. And the second is like unto it, Thou shalt love thy neighbor as thyself" (Matt. 22: 37-39). This says everything. Man can exist in God's great world only if he loves — loves his Lord and loves the creatures of the Lord. This love determines his place in the Kingdom. Love alone is the way to the *shalom.* In the demand to love our neighbor, we think first of our fellow men, but also of our relation to all the other creatures. Social life demands this, but the same demand touches all other relations. These are indeed seldom discussed separately in the Bible, but when they are it is done very clearly. "A righteous man regardeth the life of his beast" (Prov. 12:10), demonstrates God's care for plants and beasts. Psalm 104 is dedicated to God's care for beasts and plants, and Psalm 147 points out that God "giveth to the beast his food and to the young ravens which cry" (v. 9). If God regards all these creatures with so much care, it stands to reason that He expects man to deal lovingly with these fellow creatures. The "neighbor" in the great commandment is in the first place one's fellow man; but that is not all, for plants and beasts are also included.

The way in which Jesus speaks about plants and beasts, and His concern for them, are living models of the attitude He expects us to have. He speaks of the birds in the sky and the lilies of the field, and tells us that God clothes the grass of the field; and He does all this with so much love that it is very clear that He included all these creatures in His love (Matt. 6: 26). It has been told of the well-known Japanese Christian, Kagawa, that these words of Jesus made a deep impression on him when he was a child. He felt that someone who had as much love for nature as Jesus obviously had, inspires confidence immediately.

All these reasons make it obvious that the law of the Kingdom demands of every creature that he remain where the Creator has put him, and that he conform to the great harmonious pattern of all things. The apostle John fathomed this when he said, "He that loveth not knoweth not God: for God is love" (I John 4:8). It is true that the Bible does not know the thought of the *ahimsa,* which, in the radical sense, means that no living being may be killed. This is connected with the fact that man, occupying a unique place in the total plan of the world, has been given authority over the lives of animals (Gen. 9:3), but that does not mean that he may kill and torture to his heart's content. His attitude to plants and beasts also has a moral aspect. Man is allowed to exercise certain rights, but he must also respect the law of the Kingdom, and this law demands that he use his rights with respect and compassion. Man is before God's countenance even in his dealings with nature.

CRIME AND RETRIBUTION

Naturally, the law of the Kingdom also implies that every violation thereof brings disasters. God has planned this world as a community, where every creature, in accordance with his rank and ability, is set in a particular place which he is not allowed to desert. If all creatures range themselves reverently round God's throne, it means that peace, *shalom,* reigns in the world. But as soon as man, who occupied an important place in the whole of the cosmos, thoroughly perverted his relation to God when he proclaimed himself a kind of god, the *shalom* was broken, and much care and misery manifested themselves in the world. It would be reasonable to declare that this misery resulted quite automatically from the fatal violation of the order. Such a declaration would lead us immediately to the knowledge that India has known and taught for many centuries, the law of *karma. Karma* means, as we know, that our works are automatically rewarded or punished; we permanently eat the fruits of our own deeds. This law was especially applied to the succession of births. A man comes into the world in the condition and status he has made himself worthy of in his previous existence. In this life he atones for the transgressions he made in a preceding life. Well, except for this last application, we could ask the question as to whether the Bible too knows a conception which can be compared to *karma,* and as soon as we investigate this further, it strikes us that the Bible often uses expressions which strongly remind us of the concept of *karma.* Often the Bible points out that sin punishes itself in all kinds of mysterious ways. It is interesting to investigate how and where this happens.

It is at once remarkable that expressions which remind us of the concept of *karma* occur especially in the book of Proverbs and in the prophecy of Jeremiah, which teem with karmatic formulations. In Proverbs 1:18 it is said of people who live loveless and criminal lives that they "lay wait for their own blood, they lurk privily for their own lives." This means that every sin is somewhat of the nature of suicide. Man destroys his own happiness in life by violating the law of the Kingdom. Proverbs 5:22 runs as follows: "His own iniquities shall take the wicked himself, and he shall be holden with the cords of his sins." Again the same thought strikes us: Sin punishes

itself; there is a very subtle connection between sins resulting
from our character and our misery in life. Hear further from
Proverbs 11:5: "The righteousness of the perfect shall direct his
way, but the wicked shall fall by his own wickedness." Pov-
erbs 26:27 formulates this general principle as follows:
"Whoso diggeth a pit shall fall therein, and he that rolleth a
stone, it shall return upon him." Proverbs 29:23 adds this:
"A man's pride shall bring him low, but honor shall uphold
the humble in spirit."

In the prophecies of Jeremiah we find an equally large number of examples. Jeremiah 2:19 says, "Thine own wickedness
shall correct thee, and thy backslidings shall reprove thee; know
therefore and see that it is an evil thing and bitter, that thou
hast forsaken the Lord thy God." In Jeremiah 6:19 the coming disasters are mentioned as "the fruit of their own thoughts,"
and in 7:19 the question is asked whether the Israelites provoke
the Lord by their sinful behavior, or if they provoke themselves,
to their own confusion.

Although these two books of the Bible especially are full
of karmatic thoughts, they are not the only ones. In Psalm 37:
15 it is said of the wicked that "their sword shall enter into their
own heart" and in the speech of Elifaz in the book of Job we
read that "they who plow iniquity, and sow wickedness, reap
the same" (4:8).

In the New Testament the close connection between sin and
punishment is spoken of in a similar way. Jesus Himself says
in Matthew 7:12, "Judge not, that ye be not judged. For with
what judgment ye judge, ye shall be judged, and with what
measure ye mete, it shall be measured to you again." And
St. Paul expresses himself as follows in Galatians 6:7, 8, "For
whatsoever a man soweth, that shall he also reap. For he that
soweth to his flesh shall of the flesh reap corruption; but he
that soweth to the Spirit shall of the Spirit reap life everlasting." This also explains why Paul can say, when the Jews
in the small town of Antioch in Asia Minor do not listen to
him and even turn away from him, "It was necessary that the

word of God should first have been spoken to you: but seeing
ye put it from you, and judge yourselves unworthy of everlasting life, lo, we turn to the gentiles." Sin has an element of
suicide. Man, who deserts his place in God's world and makes
himself great, and pretends that he himself is a god, throws
himself in the gulf of chaos and destruction. Sin punishes itself.

Meanwhile it is certainly of importance to trace how these
karmatic-sounding words in the Bible must be understood,
and how they are related to the thought of the *karma* as we find
it in India. The first thing that strikes us in those places of
the Bible where punishment of evil is spoken of (in such a
form that it seems as if this punishment automatically results
from sin) is that the name of God is not mentioned, but that
it is nevertheless thought to be continually present. This is
especially clear because the presence of God is often expressly
mentioned. Judges 9:57 declares that "God did render all
the evil of the men of Shechem upon their own heads." This
has a karmatic effect — sin punishes itself, but in that process
God is thought to be, and is seen as, the author. This is equally
clear in Jeremiah 21:14, where God says, "I will punish you
according to the fruit of your doings." Again the karmatic
effect, the "fruit of your doings"; but again God is the cause
of it. The poet of the Lamentations of Jeremiah complains:
"The yoke of my transgressions is bound by his hand: they
are wreathed, and come upon my neck." The transgressions
again punish themselves, but "by his hand" is emphatically
added (Lam. 1:14). It often seems in this world as if the causal
connection between sin and punishment works absolutely automatically, and as if God need not come into the picture, but
this is an optical illusion. God is continually present. He causes
it all. He is hidden behind the simple phenomena, as He often
hides Himself (Is. 45:15). He likes to act through people,
or through arranging situations, or in a thousand different ways,
but He is present in them all. It is very valuable to pay attention to this, because we are always involved with God Him-

self in everything that happens to us. There exists no neutral, impersonal *karma* that just drops on us and that we cannot escape. The law of requital, too, which is often very visible in life, is never substantiated, never made a separate power, apart from God. All along, even in suffering the effect of our own deeds, we have to do personally with God. God is always involved. This also implies that we do not need to undergo the boomerang effect of our deeds fatalistically, in the supposition that no man and no god can help us. Then, too, we may count on God's forgiving and freeing grace when we seek Him and beg it of Him. Life in this world is not the laborious endurance of what an unpersonal karmatic power pours out over us, but it always remains a dialogue with God. No power breaks this dialogue, or comes in between the participants as a destructive power.

A second aspect of the biblical exposition of the law of requital is that the Bible looks upon man very much in the social and cultural relation in which he finds himself. It has been said of Indian karmatic thought that it is "utterly individualistic" and "does not take account of social solidarity." The Bible sees man much more as a being in close relation with others, in which connection too he sins and is punished. In the Bible, the concept "human race" is not just an abstraction without reality, but on the contrary it is one of the concepts forming the heart of the biblical message. As human beings, we are one. We can say of most of our faults that we make them together and that the sins of one person actively involve all others. We are not so isolated from each other that we can draw a sharp line between the *karma* of the one and that of the other. Godfrey E. Phillips dared, in his study on *The Gospel in the World,* to speak of our "collective race karma" that rests on us all, and from which Christ has redeemed us. In the Old Testament this collectivity of guilt comes more to the fore. The people of Israel are nearly always addressed as a unity. As a people, Israel has strayed, as a people it broke the covenant with Jahweh and went its own way. As a people it is afterwards punished, when hostile powers occupy its towns and lead away the inhabitants as slaves. This is indeed so much the case that the prophets, although they personally disassociate themselves from the sins of the people, identify themselves completely with the people as a whole every time. When Isaiah was called to be a prophet, he complained, "Woe is me! for I am undone; because I am a man of unclean lips, and I dwell in the midst of a people of unclean lips" (6:5). At this decisive moment of his life he knew himself to be one with his people. It is the same with the prayer of Daniel. He continually uses the word *we*: "We have sinned and have committed iniquity, and have done wickedly" (Dan. 9:5). Daniel was very conscious that we have a greater solidarity in sin than we often suppose. The New Testament accentuates more strongly the individual aspect in sin as well, but on the other hand it considers sin and punishment to be powers that have the whole world in their grasp. John the Baptist speaks of "the sin of the World" in the singular (John 1:29). There is indeed an endless variety and gradation in it, but it is, after all, one great sin, one collective revolt against God. Paul speaks in his epistle to the Romans rather at length about the difference between Jews and Gentiles, but when he comes to the positive question of whether there is a marked difference between the two as to sin he decides, "We have before proved both Jews and Gentiles, that they are all under sin." "For all have sinned, and come short of the glory of God" (Romans 3: 9, 23).

This preaching is becoming urgent again in our day. We are discovering the concept called "world history." That means, we are beginning to see that humanity is one body and that all races and all peoples form a whole. This is so important to us that we begin to feel that only together can we exist as a unity. One world or none. The faults we have made in history, and still make, were made by us all together, although there exist all kinds of shades and gradations in those faults. Together we are confronted with this great moment in world history, like frightened children who are scared of what they themselves have made.

A third point that deserves our attention is that the word *karma,* if we are to use it, needs a broadening and deepening. In Indian thinking it is generally understood as the boomerang effect, of which we have spoken, whereby our faults come home to roost and we spoil our own happiness through our wrong deeds. It seems to me that we must look at the whole concept of requital in all its intricacy. My deed wakens powers which indeed come back to me again. Proud and opinionated man forces himself into a loneliness which oppresses him after a while. Undeniably there are remarkable karmatic effects in life, effects wherein God's hand is involved in a hidden way.

But that is not all. My deed is not only a matter concerning myself, but it always has to do with social life, with my relation to nature and to the cosmos as a whole, and with my relationship to God. It is always more than the boomerang effect that comes back to myself, for we see an after-effect of our deeds in the different spheres of our existence. Human life is a most delicate, combined play of powers which develops itself in the multidimensional plan of man's relations. Man causes effects to different sides. Not only his own life undergoes this effect, but also the lives of those who are related to him, his wife, his children, and many others. The greater a man becomes, the larger the circle wherein the effect of his deeds is felt. Nature, and his existence *in* nature, are influenced by his deeds as well. But the most decisive thing is that his relation to God is continually at stake. Man is always busy with God; he flees from God or seeks Him, he struggles with God or finds Him. If we could fathom the life of man right to the bottom, we should see that the conversation with God, either in a positive or a negative sense, is the decisive theme. Man himself is generally not conscious of this, for he lives his existence on earth merely as a visit with worldly realities, with social and cosmic relations.

CHAPTER XIII

MAN'S BONDAGE

The English author Oscar Wilde once said: "Nothing is more rare in any man than an act of his own." There is a good deal of truth in this saying. Life envelops us all in such an endless chain of inescapable obligations and habits that there remains little room for deeds that are one hundred per cent our own. Especially today, with its overwhelming means of communication such as the newspaper, radio, and television, which govern our existence from day to day, man must possess a powerful personality if he is to put a personal stamp upon his life as a whole. In our language we still say that man leads his own life, but we might ask if it were not better to say that man *undergoes* his life. Is it not true that by far the greater part of our daily existence consists of totally impersonal routine events that carry us along and leave little room for us to do things on our own initiative? No wonder that many people with a clear idea of their existence feel very strongly that they are being lived, instead of living, in the active sense of the word. The Bible speaks of a king who was carried along "like a chip on the face of the waters" (Hos. 10:7). The King James Version translates: "cut off as the foam upon the water," but a better translation is "a chip," which must mean that he is "tossed about without ability to move in a definite path."[1]

It is clear that we are dealing here with one of the most important problems with which our thinking can be confronted. Or, rather, not just our thinking, but our whole existence, is at stake. It is of great importance in defining the pattern of our lives to know whether we are first of all authors, or victims, of our lives. To this question, which greatly affects our existence, every religion has sought an answer, and hence it is understandable that the Bible repeatedly deals with this problem.

The first thing that strikes us when reading the Bible is that it emphasizes the active part of human life. Man is called to active deeds in a very special sense, and it is remarkable that in the description of creation in Genesis 1, the other creatures are also depicted as being active. When God had created the waters, He said: "Let the waters swarm with swarms of living creatures" (v. 20). When God had created the earth, He said: "Let the earth bring forth living creatures after their kind." In other words, right from the very beginning God actively includes every creature He has made in the events. He makes every object at once a fellow subject. The sea and the earth become God's fellow workers.

If this holds true for impersonal creatures, it does so much more, and more directly, for man. God addresses the waters and the earth in the third person imperative; man is addressed in the second person imperative: "Replenish the earth and subdue it and have dominion." Man is distinctly addressed by God with the word "you," and because God has called him "you," man may call himself "I." Man is included in the great plan of the Creator as a fellow worker of God; he is allowed to finish God's work in many aspects; he is allowed to subject the earth and cultivate it; and he is allowed to trace the secrets of creation and think God's thoughts after Him. We could say that the

[1] W. R. Harper, *A Critical and Exegetical Commentary on Amos and Hosea.* New York: Scribners, 1905 (International Critical Commentary), p. 347.

essence of man's life is his authorship, his being God's fellow worker. In the kingdom of nature man is, as we have seen, much more than just a particle; he is God's deputy, and that means that the essence of his existence is his activity. At least this was so in the pristine Kingdom, when man still walked before God's countenance.

But all this changed through the destroying event described in Genesis 3. Man broke the tie with the Kingdom, because he desired to be as God, and so he came to be on his own, entertaining the illusion that he had received a new freedom. From that moment on bondage entered into his existence from different sources. All through the Bible this bondage is strongly emphasized.

This bondage is in the first place closely involved with the pattern of his thinking, in his view of life, man is influenced by his fellow man from his early youth. In a certain sense he is made and formed by others. The Bible presents this far more comprehensively: Humanity as a whole has fallen by the first sin. He is "brought forth in iniquity"; "And in sin did my mother conceive me," David says in Psalm 51. Man is in bondage even in birth, and no one can free himself of it.

In the second place, the Bible emphasizes that this bondage also includes the fact that man is dominated by demoniac powers. Already in Genesis 3 we read of the spell certain powers have cast on man, which mislead him and destroy his life. In Genesis 4 God says to Cain: "If thou doest not well, sin coucheth at the door; and unto thee shall be its desire" (v. 7). Human existence is not as safe as it may seem; it is continually threatened by this mysterious foe who lies "at the door." Jesus spoke about this spell of the demoniac powers later on in very serious words: "Ye are of your father the devil. . . . He was a murderer from the beginning, and standeth not in truth, because there is no truth in him" (John 8:44). Hinduism has its *maya,* the enchantment which conjures up all kinds of unreal things and which man desires. The Bible presents a sort of *maya* of a totally different nature. It is the enchantment of sin which suggests to man that being on his own, being separate from God, is the height of freedom and happiness, and hides from him the fact that loneliness and misery result from it. Paul depicts this in dark colors. He says to the Ephesians that they "once walked according to the course of this world, according to the prince of the powers of the air, of the spirit that now worketh in the sons of disobedience" (Eph. 2:2). This something that is called "the course of this world" is a seemingly impersonal movement, but demoniac powers operate behind it and man has never been aware of it. But in the Bible there is a deep awareness of this spell, and when it speaks of "salvation," it implies also deliverance from the fatal narcosis of this demoniac influence.

In the third place, man's bondage manifests itself in the fact that he is the victim of wrong habits. After he does an evil thing once, his resistance is weakened and the pressure of that evil increases. In the same chapter in which Jesus speaks of the enchantment of demoniac powers, He says: "Whosoever committeth sin is the servant of sin." Its alarming truth is not only evident in the lives of so many who are addicted to alcohol or dope or other substances, but it can be sensed in the life of every man. Psychology shows us that our daily behavior cuts grooves that eventually curtail our freedom, and causes our actions to follow these precut grooves. We may do our utmost to make a fresh start, but the burden of the past will always rest on us. We human beings are never absolutely free.

All this means that man, who left the shelter of the Kingdom because he wanted to be like God and to determine his own life, discovers that in the course of his life his freedom increasingly diminishes. This is true especially in our day. Great masses no longer obtain even a measure of personal life or a personal choice; their lives flow on, propelled, as it were, by that strange impersonal thing St. Paul calls "the course of the world." Nevertheless there remains in man that inalienable quality called his responsibility. It may be true that his behavior was pretty much decided by all kinds of powers that kept him in their grasp, nevertheless something inside him said "yes" to what these powers dictated to him. He can never run away entirely from his responsibility, at least not as long as he is not completely insane. Therefore a magistrate who must judge a criminal may take into account all kinds of considerations that excuse the crimes, but ultimately he must arrive at the man's responsibility. The criminal deserves punishment — he cannot be treated as a victim of all kinds of circumstances. Somewhere in his life he made, and still makes, a choice, and he must be judged according to that choice. Jesus, speaking about the inhabitants of Jerusalem in one of his last sermons, could have found all kinds of excuses for them. They had indeed been misled by their priests and scribes, they were fed with wrong ideas, they were governed badly, and they lived on in outdated and outworn traditions. All these Jesus could have taken into account, but He said, both in pity and in reproach: "How often would I have gathered thy children together, even as a hen gathereth her chickens under her wings, and ye would not" (Matt. 23:37). With these last words, "ye would not," Jesus treats them as responsible people who, in spite of the bondage to which they are subjected, can never be treated as things. They deserve to be treated seriously.

UNDER GOD'S GUIDANCE

The foregoing observations concern one side of man's life, his being in bondage. His being a victim is an important aspect of his life. "Nothing is rarer in any man than an act of his own."

But there is another side, and this will confront us with great riddles. We must now speak about God's guidance in connection with man's acts. Within the boundaries of the Kingdom this guidance did not pose a problem. Man's deeds were part of God's deeds; they were in keeping with God's creative work. God had made this world, and man was allowed to dominate, subdue, and cultivate it. This constituted one whole and there were no difficulties. Problems arose only when man went his own way. It is remarkable that the Bible always depicts man as being on the move. Man is by nature a traveler — he is always going somewhere. He has particular visions; he strives after a distant goal. That is why the Bible uses the word *way* so often. Again and again man is warned that he must walk in the "ways of the Lord," and he is told that these ways are safe. But it also speaks of man's "own ways," the ways he chooses himself. Paul speaks of men's "own ways," in Lystra. They are always ways in which man makes mistakes and continually misunderstands things (Acts 14:16). Man's "own ways" no longer coincide with God's way; they are not the natural consequence of God's intentions with man. The great question the Bible discusses is whether this autonomous man, who left the safe shelter of the Kingdom, who forsook God's ways and wanted to be king himself, can frustrate God's intention with the world. Is this autonomous man still subject to God's guidance? That is the problem.

The Bible gives a very definite answer, and we must consider certain points in giving this answer.

In the first place, we must keep in mind that the Bible never deals with this problem philosophically. That is outside the scope of its witness. We are concerned with the deeply religious question whether we can still trust in God's guidance of the world. Is it thwarted by human opposition? Can and may we trust that God's plan with our lives, and with the world, will be completed in spite of human opposition? This question is first mentioned clearly in the Bible, in the story of Joseph. He has been treated mercilessly, for his own brothers sold him as a slave. When at last it is clear that everything has ended well, Joseph says to his brothers: "As for you, ye meant evil against me; but God meant it for good, to bring to pass, as it is this day, to save much people alive" (Gen. 50:20). This touches the heart of the matter. People act, and they remain responsible for their acts, for the acts are theirs. But, in a way we shall never understand these acts are fitted into God's plan for the world. God's plan is not defeated by these acts; on the contrary, He uses them to reach His own object. Hence it is not surprising that the Bible touches upon this most difficult point, especially when we are confronted with important aspects of the divine plan. We have mentioned the story of Joseph because that was of great importance for the further history of the people of Israel. A later crucial moment is the exodus out of Egypt and the history of Moses. The Bible strongly emphasizes that Pharaoh's opposition to Moses, which nearly threatened to make the exodus impossible, could not change or thwart God's plan in any respect. On the contrary, the opposition of this sinful and autonomous man, who listened to no reason from any god, was a means in God's hands to reveal His great power and to smooth the way for the future. The book of Exodus presents these things in a very remarkable way. First it is repeatedly said that Pharaoh hardened his heart, that he hearkened not unto them (Ex. 7:13; 8:19; 9:7). But then suddenly we find that "Jehovah hardened the heart of Pharaoh, and he hearkened not unto them" (9:12). Suddenly God Himself is said to be the author of it all, in very strong terms. The intention of these words is probably that God made this vain and grim man walk in "his own ways" and did not check him or soften his heart. Therefore his hardening of his heart became greater and stronger. This was no disappointment to God, for God's plan was not frustrated by it. To make this very clear, it is said in terms that almost give the impression that God Himself was the cause, whereas all the while it was Pharaoh's own doing. Especially in the account of the suffering and death of Jesus Christ the emphasis is on divine guidance. There we are confronted with the heart of the gospel, where nothing depends on accidental circumstances. Therefore the crucial question is whether all the things done by people in Christ's passion are casual facts that might just as well not have happened, or whether they were all included in the divine plan. Because we are dealing here with the most central facts of the gospel, the Bible speaks very openly and clearly.

It strikes us that Jesus Himself more than once used the expression "must" in connection with His suffering. When He announced His suffering for the first time to His disciples, He said, "that he must go unto Jerusalem, and suffer many things of the elders and chief priests and scribes, and be killed, and the third day be raised up" (Matt. 16:21). That is why Jesus could say when He was taken prisoner: "The cup which the Father hath given me, shall I not drink it?" (John 18:11). He saw all these people who made Him suffer, because He knew that God Himself had included these things in His plan. Later on, the believers in Jerusalem expressed themselves in prayer in the same manner: "For of a truth in this city against thy holy Servant Jesus, whom thou didst anoint, both Herod and Pontius Pilate, with the Gentiles and the peoples of Israel, were gathered together, to do whatsoever thy hand and thy counsel foreordained to come to pass" (Acts 4:27). Again and again it is emphasized that the events which took place were no surprise to God. They did not interfere with His intention; on the contrary, they were included in it. The people who performed the acts acted according to their own views and their own responsibility, but they could not frustrate God's holy intentions. The basic idea is that although man has left the boundaries of God's Kingdom and is on his own, and although in this aeon God's Kingship of the world is shrouded in mist and haze, God is nevertheless Lord. The Psalms proclaim: "The Lord reigneth!"

The history of the world seen from this perspective takes on a different aspect. To be sure, dreadful powers arraign themselves against God in world history, but their might never becomes so great that God is threatened by them. The prophet Daniel saw them, as it were, rising from the rough sea of the masses of world-conquering nations, but the situation never once escaped God's grasp. He remained sovereign, and He governed all. Israel's faith in this helped the people spiritually through the days of the destruction of Jerusalem and the anxious years of exile. The prophets of those days struggled with the question of how it was possible that the Lord used proud and heathen Babylon to chastise His people. Was not Babylon much more wicked and dreadful than Israel itself? Jeremiah, too, struggled for a moment with the fear that wicked Babylon would destroy Israel as soon as it could do so. But he comforted himself with the knowledge "that the way of man is not in himself; it is not in man that walketh to direct his steps." The king of Babylon could go no further than God allowed. Therefore Jeremiah could continue: "O, Jehovah, correct me, but in measure; not in thine anger, lest thou bring me to nothing" (Jer. 10:23). God had given His sword into the hand of the king of Babylon for a little while, but He Himself held the hand of the king. God's children, as they take their place in world history, are before God's countenance every moment.

It needs no argument that these thoughts do not solve the great riddle of human life. But it is clear that we can never maintain that man is merely a victim of unknown, all-dominating powers. He is the author of his own deeds, although his freedom is very limited and he is subject to powers stronger than he. He is the author, but at the same time all his acts are under God's rule in a way which he does not fathom and which will always remain untraceable. Man cannot thwart God's plan, for God assimilates man's acts and thus carries out His plan with the world. The Bible never goes to the trouble of making this mystery philosophically acceptable, but from every page it can be sensed that our rest and safety depend on this truth. We are in God's hand in spite of all the upheavals in world history.

CHAPTER XIV

SALVATION AND THE KINGDOM

For those who divide the religions of the world into soteriological religions and legalistic religions it is an established fact that the Christian religion must be considered a soteriological religion. In the Christian religion the idea of redemption is not just one of several elements, but it is the heart of it. We are dealing here with the redemption by Jesus Christ.

In speaking of the soteriological religions someone may also mention the Indian religious systems in the same breath with Christianity. For in Hinduism, too, and especially in Buddhism, salvation is one of the main ideas. For millions of Hindus the belief in the striving after *moksha,* salvation, is one of the most essential features of their religion. A person may take different *margas,* ways, to reach salvation, but the final object always remains the same. In this world of unreality we search for reality; in this world of instability we search for stability. Somewhere there must be a great "beyond," something above and beyond death and labor and poverty. The Vedanta defined this "beyond" as being one with Brahman, as submerging in the ocean of his glory. In Buddhism the word *nirwana* is used for absolute salvation. Judging from the sound of it, this is a purely negative conception, as it means "being extin-

guished," but for many adherents of this religion it is the syno-
nym of "bliss unspeakable."

Now, it is possible to use the Indian word for redemption
when preaching the gospel of Jesus Christ in India, and to
speak of the *moksha* through Christ. But then this word gets
a totally different meaning from the different context in which
it is placed. Therefore it is quite important to examine what
exactly the word *redemption* means in the Bible. As soon as
we get a clear idea of this, it becomes obvious that the idea of
redemption is closely connected with that of the Kingdom of
God. The Kingdom itself is salvation. Jesus always spoke of
it in connection with "regeneration," because entering the Kingdom implies a new birth, the birth of a new cosmos (Matt. 19:
38). In the Acts of the Apostles the word "restoration of all
things" is used (Acts 3:21). That means that this damaged
world in which all order is lost and where the powers of chaos
reign, will be, as Paul expresses it, gathered together again.
Whenever the Bible touches upon salvation, it actually means
ultimate regeneration. Salvation has, by its very nature, cosmic
dimensions. There is not such a thing as individual happiness
— all true happiness is necessarily social, and it includes other
people and ultimately the whole world. In the Old Testament
this ultimate redemption is generally regarded as the result of a
long process of wars and destruction. From the very ocean,
the symbolic representation of humanity, new kingdoms rise
up continually, which always have bestial traits and assault
weak and defenseless people. This process goes on until at last
the Lord will intervene and usher in the new Kingdom, the
Kingdom of the Son of man. Often it is said that at the end
of time the hostile powers will turn to Jerusalem, the holy
city, for a final battle, but in this last and most violent war
of all the Lord Himself will give the victory. Each eschatological vision always ends in marvelous beauty and great serious-
ness. It is said in tender words that the peoples will come
spontaneously to the people of the Lord and will bow down

before Him. Isaiah describes how God "in this mountain will make unto all peoples a feast of fat things . . . , and he will destroy in this mountain the face of the covering that covereth all peoples, and the veil that is spread over all nations" (Is. 25: 6). And that will be the end, the salvation of God's community.

Quite naturally the question arises, What is salvation, and from what must we be redeemed? Upon closer reflection it becomes evident that the Bible differs greatly from all the other holy books of humanity. It is very difficult to describe exactly what this mysterious thing is that dooms the world to confusion and destruction. We can best describe it as the guilt of man. The one sinful act of man violated something so that all fundamental relations are disturbed. The Psalmist in Psalm 82, complaining about the unjust judges who pass judgment according to their own pleasure, says: "All the foundations of the earth are shaken" (v. 5). That is what happened through man's sin. The moral order of the world is so essential that a violation of it can only mean a complete destruction of all relations. Man is guilty before God. If the Bible emphasizes one thing in connection with this guilty relation, it is that God cannot possibly act as if nothing had happened. We could speak here of divine impotence which the Bible itself speaks of in II Timothy 2:13 — God "cannot deny himself"; He is what He is. Something very essential was violated in the original relationship between God and man, and that is the cause of all misery in the world. All attempts of man to redeem himself are hopeless in view of this violation. There is no self-deliverance, no means of freeing oneself from the claims of guilt. There are no *margas,* no ways by which man can find the lost Paradise again. The curse that rests on his existence on account of having lost God, and of "having no hope and without God in the world" (Eph. 2:12), cannot be undone by himself. Man's history is extremely tragic throughout.

It is in this connection that the Bible speaks of salvation

through Jesus Christ. Man must somehow feel the uselessness of every attempt, if he is to understand something of the wonder of Jesus Christ. We cannot put Him on a level with the *avataras,* the "descenders," in Hinduism. *Avataras* are figures that come down to earth in great moments of tension, when lawlessness and confusion increase, to restore justice and order. Jesus Christ is different. In Him, God Himself enters into this world to reconcile the world unto Himself by the great sacrifice of Jesus Christ (II Cor. 5:19).

The cross is shrouded in fathomless mystery. No man can grasp what happened there. The Church has always confessed with the prophet Isaiah: "All we like sheep have gone astray; we have turned every one to his own way; and Jehovah hath laid on him the iniquity of us all" (Is. 53:6). The incomprehensible love of God to us human beings, who have strayed far from Him, comes to us in Jesus Christ. If we wish to speak of a *marga,* a way, then we must think of the *marga* which God Himself has given us in Jesus Christ. Through Him a new contact with God is possible; through Him we, who have sunk so deeply, can find Him who wants to be the Light of our lives.

Hence the answer to the question: What is it from which we must be redeemed? is: From our guilt. This guilt implies a broken connection, it means that no communication, in the full sense of the word, was possible any more; it also means that since we lost God, we had to live out our weary lives in a cursed world.

It is clear that this guilt had many more adverse results. The Bible speaks in this connection of our being subject to the power of Satan. Demoniac powers have dominion over the life of the world. In our restless and anxious age, we can better imagine these demoniac powers than could preceding generations who could regard life with careless optimism. Although we may be loathe to admit it, we must be convinced that our civilization, highly developed as it may be, suffers from an incurable disease which we cannot possibly conquer. Fear of the senselessness of our creating and working grips us. This fear comes to expression in our literature. The nightmare of "the brave new world" is one of the characteristic phenomena of our age. Mankind is relentlessley being driven on, and continually creates new possibilities; and new civilizations rise up. Yet an oppressive cloud hangs over it. Sometimes it seems as if this whole process will ultimately result in wholesale destruction, because mankind just cannot build a society that really (and in the full sense of the word) *bears the characteristics* of what the Bible calls *shalom*. The Bible expresses the senselessness of all these things very movingly: "The broad walls of Babylon shall be utterly overthrown, and her high gates shall be burned with fire; and the peoples shall labor for vanity, and the nations for the fire; and they shall be weary" (Jer. 51: 58). It could not be expressed more accurately.

Nevertheless the Bible is certainly not a pessimistic book. One expression occurs again and again in the Bible: "The Lord will turn thy fortune." (Formerly this expression was translated "turn thy captivity," but nowadays preference is given to the more general translation, "turn thy fortune.") This expression indicates that what we call world history is more than just a one-sided monologue from us, the human race, but that right through it God is unfolding His restorative plan. Time and again He comes to us with His help and the proofs of His love. This shows that there is room in world history for the decisive "turning" which only God can bring about, and which He has already brought about. This turning finds its climax in the resurrection of Christ from the dead. There a wholly new aeon begins, the aeon of God's salvation. Through the resurrection of Christ, dejected apostles are made courageous and dedicated men who bring the message of salvation to the world. Through their witness of the resurrection, their world experienced the great "turn." The Roman Empire is shaken to its foundations, and a Church develops which dares to hope

in ultimate redemption while surrounded by oppression and diffi-
culty. From that moment history changed. There is still much
darkness; there are still wars and nameless cruelty and terror;
but God's turning can be seen again and again. Sometimes
we see it only in the lives of a few people who have experienced the great turning of conversion and have become entirely different. Sometimes we see that with the change God
causes in the lives of men, social conditions change too, so
that people of different races join at one table for Holy Communion. Since the first Easter World, history is no longer
the senseless struggle "for nothing." The power of this "turning" changes it into something fascinating that continually fills
us with great expectations in spite of all the remaining gloom.

By way of summary, we can say the following about salvation: (1) Salvation means first of all that the guilt that rested
on man and made him God's enemy and a slave of the demoniac
powers has been taken away by the wholly mysterious event
of the suffering and death and resurrection of Jesus Christ.
The Bible sometimes uses the word "justification" for salvation: "Being justified by faith, we have peace with God through
our Lord Jesus Christ" (Rom. 5:1). There is a new relation
to God. The tension between Him and us has been removed.
We may once again approach Him as our Father in heaven.
But through this change the world and life have completely
changed as well (in its *radix,* i.e., in its root). The former
fear has vanished. "We know that to them that love God all
things work together for good" (Rom. 8:28). This reveals
itself in one's personal life. Man individually receives this
salvation from God as a gift that makes all things new through
Jesus Christ.

Among the Hindus there are certain people who are called
jivan mukta, i.e., those who have already found the secret of
salvation in this life. We could use this word — but in an
entirely different sense — for those who believe in Jesus Christ.
They are *jivan mukta,* that is to say, although they still belong

to this world and occupy their place in it as sinful men, they are already citizens of the new Kingdom and so already possess the great secret of the *shalom,* since God brought about the "turning" into their lives through Jesus Christ. Paul says, "We are citizens of heaven" (Phil. 3:20). Although we still belong to this aeon, in essence we have been lifted above it.

(2) Salvation further implies a new attitude in life. In principle the bondage is broken. Jesus says: "If therefore the Son shall make you free, ye shall be free indeed" (John 8:36). The word "freedom," which has always enchanted man, gets a new meaning through the change that God brings into the life of man. This does not mean that all sinful inclinations suddenly stop, but it does mean that a new power has penetrated man, the power of the Holy Spirit, which makes him new and free.

This change also implies a new vocation. Man suddenly sees the course of his life; his life receives a new goal and a new meaning. He must now direct his life towards the Kingdom; the *shalom* of the Kingdom must now determine his conduct. In the light of this, his relation to his fellow men changes radically. They are no longer his rivals, his competitors. Fear and indifference leave him. He begins to understand the Sermon on the Mount, in which Jesus outlines life in the Kingdom. Even loving one's enemies is no longer impossible when one has been touched by the love of Christ. A new society must be created, and social life must be renewed through individual lives. The change in the heart of man must lead to a change in the community. When that takes place, circumstances, too, lose something of their force. A citizen of the Kingdom receives a certain independence from prosperity and adversity, illness and death. Paul says: "I am persuaded, that neither death, nor life, nor angels, nor principalities, nor things present, nor things to come, nor height, nor depth, nor any other creature, shall be able to separate us from the love of God, which is in Christ Jesus our Lord" (Rom. 8:38). The threat has vanished. Circumstances such as prosperity and adversity are no longer decisive. It is now possible to be happy even in the greatest trouble, through the Lord.

(3) These changes concern individual man and his place in the world. We have already noted that individual man can never be seen as separated from the cosmos as a whole. Hence salvation implies more than the redemption of individual men. The world as a whole shares in the enormous change which God brings about and which started with the resurrection of Christ. Here the mighty perspectives unfold which we touched upon on a few previous occasions — the perspectives of *shalom,* when homicide and hatred will disappear, and of the unification of all things when all things will be gathered together in Christ. The Revelation of John unfolds this perspective before our eyes, when it speaks of a new heaven and a new earth: "for the first heaven and the first earth are passed away" (21:1).

From this it is clear that salvation has at once both personal and cosmic dimensions; that it is already fact and at the same time belongs to the *eschata,* the last things; that it not only involves a complete change in all relations but that it also includes the entire man in body and soul. One cannot use the word "salvation" without touching upon all the aspects of human life. This salvation is the work of God in the most complete sense. We are saved. But, just as in creation, when God made every object his fellow worker right from the very beginning, we see the same thing here. Redeemed man is concerned with God's plan of salvation right from the beginning. That is why Paul boldly describes himself and his fellow workers as people who "share in God's work" (II Cor. 6:1), as ambassadors for Christ. The devout Moslem divides the world into two realms, the *dār al-harb,* the realm of war, and the *dār al Islam,* the realm where the holy law of Allah is reverently acknowledged and obeyed. Therefore the faithful must fight the *jihād,* the war of the way of Allah. The Christian has this obligation too, namely, to fight the weaponless combat of the way of God. This combat is a war inside his own heart against the "old man," as the New Testament calls it; at the same time it is a struggle for improving social relations. He is a servant of Jesus Christ and knows that he must prove himself to be a man who has been touched by the love of Christ and who lives out of this love.

CHAPTER XV

GOD AND THE WORLD

The final question that demands attention in this connection is, Who or what is the background of this amazing world? Must we speak of a "he," a "she," or an "it"? Do we have to do with a personal God (male or female), or do we meet with an eternal, impersonal being, a primeval ocean from which all originates? We have seen in the history of religion that there is a certain hesitancy to answer this fundamental question. In India we definitely find belief in a personal god, Ishvara (Lord), but it always seems that there is a vague notion that this Ishvara is at the same time the impersonal Brahman, the undifferentiated primeval foundation of all beings. In China we find belief on the one hand in Shang-ti, the supreme god, but on the other hand in *t'ien,* heaven, which is thought to be an impersonal power occupying the supreme place in people's minds. In Islam the personal aspect of Allah is indeed emphasized. Allah is the great King whose will we must obey. But Islamic mysticism emphasizes Dhat, the absolute Essence, or the "dark mist" or "blindness" (*al Ama*).[1] All these concepts seem to point to impersonal and undifferentiated deities.

---

[1] Nicholson, *Studies in Islamic Mysticism,* pp. 89, 94.

Hence throughout the history of religion we find this characteristic uncertainty. All over the world God is thought to be a person, a king, a father; but at the same time we see that the I-thou relation, our relation to him, is merely an aspect of a much greater and vaguer relation.

Rudolf Otto, who has deeply penetrated this question, in his study on *The Sacred* states the opinion that "the Jahveh of the Old Testament, too, is more than a God in a personal sense." He thinks the Old Testament contains thoughts that indicate that God was also known as an impersonal power. According to him, this thought is also expressed in the plural name *Elohim,* "gods": "In the beginning Elohim created heaven and earth." Otto then concludes that Jahveh is the *numen,* the mysterious *ruah,* the wind, that blows where it will. So he concludes: "Our God too is more than only God."[2] In other words, Otto assumes that the same hesitation which Buddhism, Hinduism, and virtually all religions evidence is also noticeable in the Bible.

IS GOD A PERSONAL GOD?

When we reverently approach this question, it strikes us that it is very difficult to say much about it. The reason is that our concept *person* implies all kinds of limitations. As soon as we speak about God, we notice that we must use this concept in a much higher sense than we can understand. Otto uses *das Überpersönliche* in this case. It is not difficult to explain this on the basis of the following considerations: First, the theology of the Christian Church speaks of the triune God on the basis of what the Bible teaches. It declares that the one, everlasting, and divine Being consists of three persons, the Father, the Son, and the Holy Spirit. This formulation shows that the word *person* as applied to God renders only very imperfectly what God says concerning Himself. We can speak

---

2 Rudolph Otto, *Das Heilige.* 8. aufl. Breslau: Trewendt und Gramer, 1922, pp. 273ff.

about God only in anthropomorphous terms, of which the word *person* is one. Of course, this does not imply that we may not apply this concept to God, but it does mean that if we do, we must realize that we thereby say something that applies to Him in an infinitely higher sense than we can even suppose.

This becomes at once evident when we realize what the concept *person* means in our own language. It means that two people, two "persons," are related in such a way that each of them has an independent and separate existence. Children, although they are born of parents, have become "independent persons." They call themselves "I," and this indicates that they realize that they are independent beings. They do need the help and care of parents every day, but their existence as such is no longer dependent on the parents. Even if the latter die, the children live on. Each child is a world of its own; each has its own world; each is a person. This indicates that we touch upon unfathomable mysteries when we call God a *person*. For that may imply that creation as creation and man as man exist more or less independently of God. Two persons can never overlap each other, they are always isolated from each other. If God were a "person" in this sense, the same relationship would obtain between God and man. But the very fact that the Bible can say that in him "we live and move and have our being" (Acts 17:28) and that "of him, and through him, and unto him, are all things" (Rom. 11:36) shows us that the relation between God and man is always different from that between two "persons." In spite of our being persons, we are at each moment wholly dependent upon God, and without Him we cannot exist for one second.

We must be aware of the depth of the mystery that confronts us. Man must hesitate when he is about to say something about God's being. Kraemer speaks a great truth when he says, "Not the mystery of His being or essence is revealed, because that remains God's exclusive domain, but His redemptive will towards mankind. God's saving Will, become manifest in divine action, is what is revealed in the Christian faith."[3] We may call God a person. That is neither a lie nor an error. The whole Bible makes it clear that we may do so, provided we realize that this is not an adequate but only an analogous designation. As soon as we apply the word *person* to God, this concept receives an infinitely greater meaning than it generally has. Meanwhile we must remember that it is not we who took the liberty to call God a person, but that He Himself in His revelation always describes His relation to us as that of one person to another. He is the divine I, the Creator, the Originator, the King, the Father, and we are the created ones, those who are being addressed. He speaks of Himself as I or Me. He calls us *thou*. The whole Bible depicts the relation between Him and us in this fashion. Right to the last page, He is presented as the calling, saving God and we as the saved ones, the children.

The Bible here and there hints that in the coming Kingdom, in the great "regeneration" of the whole cosmos, it will be different again, because God will then be "all in all," *panta,* all things in all (I Cor. 15:28). But there, too, the relationship still bears the characteristics of an I-thou relation. And in this new dispensation our whole life with God will be a matter of our continually being addressed by Him and His being addressed by us, when He enters our existence as our King and Lord, saving and blessing us.

The above-mentioned matters are of greater importance than we may think at first glance. As soon as the relation of God to man is no longer in the personal sphere and is thought to be a relation between the small, human *I* and the great, ineffable *It,* the primeval ocean from which we originated, religious life as a whole is completely changed. Then the principal idea of religious life is changed. Serving God is then no longer of the greatest importance, but rather to be drowned in the divine ocean and suffused with His greatness. It means that in

3 Kraemer, *The Christian Message . . . ,* p. 73.

human life the word *I* gets another connotation. It is then a delusion; it means being senselessly split off from infinity. Ultimately happiness and complete religious surrender are then sought in a dionysian ecstasy.

For this reason, mysticism, not only Indian mysticism but also other kinds all over the world, preaches so insistently of the necessity to abandon oneself. Moslem mysticism formulated it thus: "Take one step out of thyself, that thou mayest arrive at God." The idea is stated thus: "To pass away from self *(fana)* is to realise that self does not exist, and that nothing exists except God *(tawhid)*."[4] That lower "self," the *aham* (I), must be conquered by the higher "self," the *atman.* Thus the whole tension between God and us is reduced to one inside my own being. The whole drama is enacted within the two poles inside myself. All religious concepts are changed into psychological concepts. The pilgrimage to Mecca becomes a pilgrimage to man's innermost soul, to the precipices of man's own being, the *kibla;* the direction of prayer is to the innermost being of man. Karl Barth says of mysticism, that in essence it is nothing but atheism: "Mysticism, too, although it goes about it more carefully than atheism, ultimately has, in a special and concrete way, as its goal the negation of the religious upperworld. . . . Mysticism is esoteric atheism."[5] He means to say that, by relating everything to man's inmost soul, mysticism finally ends in man himself. The final result is that, in spite of the fact that the miserable *I* is spoken of in the most humble terms, there always remains the danger of a vague, subtle deification of man. We may be impressed by the words of contempt and scorn which the great mystics heap upon the human *I,* but nevertheless we have to conclude with Augustine, writing about the Greek-Roman literature of his days, that "On the pages of those writings nothing is said of the manifestations of true godliness,

4 Nicholson, *op. cit.,* p. 50.
5 Barth, *Kirchliche Dogmatik,* I, sec. 2, p. 50.

of the tears of confession, of Thy sacrifices — a broken spirit,
a broken and contrite heart."[6]

The great question — whether we may refer to the relation
between man and God as an I-Thou relation or whether we
must picture Him as an endless, impersonal ocean — not only
involves metaphysical problems that quite naturally are far
beyond our comprehension, but also jeopardizes man's very
existence. God always addresses us with *thou,* and He Himself
approaches us throughout His Word as the divine *I.* The Bible,
moreover, emphasizes that impersonal nature, too, mountains,
seas, rivers, and fields, all tell us of God. It is remarkable
with how many creatures God compares Himself. He is described as a sun and as a shield, as a lion and as the dew (Hos.
14:6), as a cypress (Hos. 14:9), and as an eagle (Deut. 32:
11); but when He wants to express what He is to us, He
appears in Jesus Christ: "The effulgence of his [God's] glory
and the very image of his substance" (Heb. 1:3). He is the
Logos in whom God reveals Himself to us, for whoever has
seen Him, has seen the Father (John 14:9). The Christian
Indian V. Chakrarai, speaking of Jesus Christ, expresses it
thus: "Out of the infinite nebulousness emerges the face of
Jesus. He who sits on the throne of the universe has the human face divine of Jesus."[7]

FATHER OR MOTHER?

A totally different question is, whether we must picture
God first of all as a father or as a mother. We have seen
that female deities play an important part in countless religions. A mother-goddess is felt to be closer to us; she is
more one with us and shares our distress. Therefore all over
the world mother-goddesses are invoked first of all as com-
forters in days of trouble. Man has the subconscious idea
that a mother-goddess makes him feel less guilty. Apparently

---

6 Augustine, *Confessiones,* VII, 21.
7 V. Chakrarai, *Jesus the Avatar.* Madras: 1926, p. 222.

she is looked upon as a deity that does not take our sin quite
as seriously as a father-god would, and understandingly smiles
down on it with motherly tenderness. The mother-goddess is
often a personification of the all-bearing earth, dark and at
the same time fruitful, from which all life emerges. We emanate
from her and will return to her in death. Some people represent their graves as a womb. The figurative, poetic expression
in Job 1:21, "Naked came I out of my mother's womb, and
naked shall I return thither," is felt to be real in some religions,
inasmuch as the womb is really identical to the bowels of the
earth. We could say that in these religions the I-you relation is
maintained, but at the same time softened. The mother-goddess
is indeed a person, an "I" over against our own "I," but she
is more identical to us, or at any rate closer to us, than a
father-god. In this connection we may point out that in some
Roman Catholic countries the Virgin Mary has taken the place
of the mother-goddess in the minds of the very simple. The
well-known secretary of the American Bible Society, Dr. E. A.
Nida, says regarding some parts of South America: "Where
the virgin is worshipped she is usually merely a fertility goddess, and in some regions of Ecuador may be taken out of her
shrine and publicly whipped if the crops do not mature properly."[8] The fact that there is always a strange temptation on
the part of man to think of God as a mother-figure may be
the reason why the Bible speaks of God as a father, and
shrinks from the word *mother*. However, this idea is not entirely absent in the Bible. It is already implied in the well-
known words of Genesis 1:7: "And God created man in his
own image, in the image of God created he him; male and
female created he them." This definitely implies that woman
bears God's image just as man does. We can say that both
man and woman, in their diversity, express God's image. In

[8] E. A. Nida, in *Bulletin of the United Bible Societies*. Third quarter,
1961, p. 106.

this sense there is really no objection to comparing God with a mother.

Another occurrence may be found in Isaiah 66:13: "As one whom his mother comforteth, so will I comfort you; and ye shall be comforted in Jerusalem." In the Parable of the Lost Coin, Jesus compares God to a woman who crawls over the floor of her house to find the lost coin. In the same way God crawls, as it were, over this world to find His lost child. God has a feminine quality — something that is motherly and tender and caring. One may acknowledge all this and at the same time feel that it is not without reason that God reveals Himself as a father in heaven, but generally not as a mother.

The name *father,* however, can also lead to misconceptions. A father may be thought to be too high, too severe, too far away. That has often occurred in the Christian Church and it has done serious damage to religious life. God was often thought of as a severe judge, and His grace and inconceivable mercy were overlooked. In such times it is good to point out that the woman, the mother, too, was created in God's image and that therefore we may always regard God at the same time as a mother. But as soon as this idea is overemphasized, it leads to another distortion of God's image. Then the idea of sin becomes blurred and relaxed; and the fact that God is completely different, and that we may never think or feel that He to some extent is identical to us, is in danger of receding into the background. The word *Father* with which we invoke God in the prayer Jesus taught us, contains at the same time the idea that God is a mother as well. This is not a contradiction. The only thing God warns us about is that, when we see Him first of all as a mother, we take dangerous risks, as the history of religion shows clearly again and again.

The Bible speaks of God in very childlike symbols. Many essentially human things are said of Him. The Bible contains a great deal of what we usually call anthropomorphism. That is because, in relation with Him, we know ourselves to be children, little children, who in this world of unfathomable mysteries search for Him and love Him with a simple heart. There simply are things that are hidden "from the wise and prudent" and "revealed unto babes" (Matt. 11:25). But on the other hand the Bible often speaks of God in exalted words, words that can only evoke great reverence and adoration. I am thinking of the well-known words in Psalm 90:2: "Before the mountains were brought forth, Or ever thou hadst formed the earth and the world, Even from everlasting to everlasting, thou art God," and I am reminded of Amos 5:8: "Seek him that maketh the Pleiades and Orion, and turneth the shadow of death into the morning, and maketh the day dark with night: that calleth for the waters of the sea, and poureth them out upon the face of the earth (Jehovah is his name)." Throughout the entire Bible resounds a tone of holy reverence. Yet it is a book that speaks to little children and in which children feel at home. And it is a book that brings us on our knees and makes us tremble before the greatness of Him who holds our life and breath in His hands.

CHAPTER XVI

THE CHURCH AND ITS MESSAGE

In some parts of the world the Church has found a place alongside the temple or the mosque. That means that it comes daily in contact with other religions and must justify itself to the adherents of the other religions. As a rule it is in the minority and has great trouble maintaining its position. Sometimes its neighbors look down upon it with contempt or even a certain hostility. For it is seen as the great spoil-sport that destroyed the people's former unity and does not want to adapt itself to the nation's way of life. Moreover, the tenacity with which the Christian Church maintains its confession of faith is sometimes regarded as a result of the guidance it supposedly receives from the so-called Western world. Mission work is looked upon as a symptom of the colonial and imperialistic tendencies of the Western world of the last centuries. Politically and economically the Western nation tried to dominate the other continents. Not being satisfied with this, they, moreover, made serious attempts to influence other parts of the world spiritually in order to acquire an even more unassailable hegemony. Politically, this gigantic enterprise proved a complete failure. The colonial nations freed themselves from their bonds. In economic life the West still has the advantage. The so-called "young" churches in Africa and Asia are still a reminder of what came into existence in the colonial period. No wonder the Church is looked upon with some suspicion in many countries.

In the midst of these conditions the Church has to decide on its attitude to temple and mosque. In this confrontation it naturally meets with different attitudes. In the first place, it encounters opposition. The other religions, Islam, Hinduism, and Buddhism, are all passing through a period of resurgence at the moment. They all went through a certain crisis in the preceding century when they came in contact with Western civilization, but they have adapted themselves to the new circumstances. This resurgence owes its impetus to a new orientation. The old traditions simply could not be maintained as before, and the leaders were compelled to chart new courses. In India it was felt that the old religion had been too static and that too much emphasis had been placed on detachment as the highest religious duty. One of the spokesmen of the new approach, Swami Vivekananda, expressed the new need as follows: "What our country now wants are muscles of iron and nerves of steel. . . . It is a man-making religion that we want."[1] Vivekananda thinks that Hinduism will be equal to this new task if it understands that it is time to speak of "the lion of Brahman." Nehru actually said the same thing, though in more secular terminology: "We have to get rid of that narrowing religious outlook, that obsession with the supernatural and metaphysical speculations. We have to come to grips with the present, this life, this world, this nature which surrounds us in its infinite variety. India must therefore lessen the religiosity and turn to science."[2] The same phenomenon we observe in Hinduism — namely, the desire to make its own religion dynamic — is also noticeable in Buddhism. In a book published in 1953, the following conclusion is drawn after a

[1] Nicol Macnicol, *The Living Religions of the Indian People*. London: SCM Press, 1934, p. 119.

[2] Nehru, *The Disovery of India*, p. 459.

circumstantial investigation of the trend of the religious revival today:

> If the religious revival is to be a genuine expression of the aspirations of the coming generation, if it is to be the force which can pour into the minds and hearts of young men and women the energy which will be required of them, it must capture a wider conception than has been attained by existing religions. We must cease to identify religion with asceticism or pietism. We must know it as embracing all the avenues of experience, we must recognize that the scientist, the physician, the artist, the politician, the industrial worker, has as much a place in the pantheon of sainthood — because their tasks are essentially religious — as the bhikku, priest or prophet.[3]

All kinds of changes are taking place in the religions of the world. Islam, too, has for some decades been involved in a process of new orientation. There, too, we find the brave attempt to acquire an openness to the modern world. One of the great leaders in this movement, Sir Mohammed Iqbal, says, "The truth is that the religious and the scientific processes, though involving different methods, are identical in their final aim. Both aim at reaching the most real."[4] In Japan, several new religions have begun to flourish since the Second World War. All these movements have this in common: they wish to reinterpret the old religions so that they act energizingly upon the life of today; and amidst this fermentation we see the Church. Outsiders always reproach the Church with attacking man's tendency to self-reliance, because its first statement is always that we are sinful men who of ourselves can do nothing. It is reproached with still maintaining in this enlightened age such metaphysical suppositions as the virgin birth of Jesus. It is reproached with having been the cause of sharp disputes and even of religious wars and persecutions in those parts of the world where it was the dominating power. The Church

---

3 *The Revolt in the Temple.* Colombo: 1953, p. 666.
4 Sir Mohammad Iqbal, *The Reconstruction of Religious Thought in Islam.* London: Oxford University Press, 1934, p. 185.

is, according to many people, the least suitable agency to guide men to a new aeon and a new world. Is it not faced these days with an alarming crisis even in the countries where it is solidly rooted? Indeed, the first reaction the Church encounters is one of fierce opposition against its message.

The second reaction is the tendency to consider all religions as equal. This syncretistic tendency manifests itself in most parts of the world. In the Far East it has always been very strong. The idea behind this tendency was that ultimate reality is so elusive and so inexpressible that every attempt to formulate it must necessarily be a poor one. This means that every religious idea gives expression only to a particular aspect of the ultimate reality and therefore can never lay claim to giving a complete picture of it. Mahatma Gandhi, the great spokesman of this viewpoint, said:

> Religions are different roads converging to the same point. What does it matter that we take different roads, so long as we reach the same goal . . . ? If a man reaches the heart of his own religion, he has reached the heart of the others too. . . . After long study and experience, I have come to the conclusion that (1) all religions are true; (2) all religions have some error in them; (3) all religions are almost as dear to me as my own Hinduism, inasmuch as all human beings should be as dear to one as one's own close relatives.[5]

This syncretistic tendency involves a willingness to leave room for the gospel of Jesus, provided the Church be ready to acknowledge that Jesus is only one prophet among others, a "descent" (*avatara*) alongside other *avataras.* Islam has always looked upon Jesus as one of the greatest prophets, and among the newer movements there are people who are willing to stress this belief even more strongly than before. They are ready to acknowledge that Jesus, too, revealed Allah's will in a very special way and must therefore be greatly honored, just as Mohammed is. Hinduism is equally ready to give

---

[5] *All Men Are Brothers; Life and Thoughts of Mahatma Gandhi as Told in His Own Words.* Paris: UNESCO, 1958, pp. 59, 60.

Jesus a place and to honor Him. Again, Gandhi confessed that he also regarded Jesus as a manifestation of God, but not as the only one — "I don't place Him upon a solitary throne." In India there are many people who gladly confess today that Jesus has revealed certain aspects of God, as an *avatara,* and that no other *avatara* has done this so clearly. In the long series of descents of God Jesus has His own place, a place which is very important, especially in the present-day world.

This is how the Church stands between temple and mosque. It cannot avoid dialogue with them. It is not sufficient merely to witness, because it will somehow have to say what it thinks of these other religions, and also of science as the great "substitute" for all religion. The Church knows that it will meet opposition, but it cannot withdraw from the discussion. It is gratifying that today in several parts of the world conversations are regularly held between Christians and leading figures of other religions. The great encounter must take place, which demands the utmost care on the part of the Church. It is very well possible that the opposition the Church meets is not as dangerous as the seeming recognition it receives from the syncretistic movements. The kind admittance that Jesus also deserves a place and that He must be respected as one of the religious leaders of humanity may have a paralyzing effect on the preaching of the gospel. It may work like a slow poison that sucks away the Church's strength. But whatever the Church may meet, it is clear that it has the duty to speak honestly and with dignity with the other religions.

THE WITNESS OF THE CHURCH

What must the Church say? What does it have to say about these other religions? And what must it answer to the remark that all religions are the same, and that "if a man reaches the heart of his own religion, he has reached the heart of the others too"? Reflecting on this, it is clear that we must begin with the two ideas expressed by Paul in Romans 1. We saw that there it is said that God has always revealed Himself to every man from the very beginning of the world. God concerns Himself with every man. Buddha would never have meditated on the way of salvation if God had not touched him. Mohammed would never have uttered his prophetic witness if God had not concerned Himself with him. Every religion contains, somehow, the silent work of God.

We have seen that man has always repressed this silent work of God. In this connection we recall the two forces Paul mentions, namely, repression and substitution. They show their pernicious strength everywhere. The Church can confess this quietly and honestly, because it judges *itself* with this confession. It is conscious that it has often been guilty of repression and substitution in the course of its history, and it also knows that its guilt in this respect is much greater than that of the other religions, because it has so often obscured the revealed and clear gospel of Jesus Christ behind all kinds of cunning, human reasonings. In other words, the Church can say these things without any pride. Every Christian knows that he is always apt to hide the truth by his own unrighteousness, and that only God's grace has taught him to acknowledge and confess this as sin. With such humility the Church can give its testimony in the world of the other religions. As I have said elsewhere, "As long as I laugh at what I regard as being foolish superstition in other religions, I look down upon the adherents of them." Then "I have not yet found the key to his [another religion's adherent's] soul. As soon as I understand that what he does in a noticeably naive and childish manner, I also do and continue to do again and again in a different form; as soon as I actually stand next to him, I can in the name of Christ stand in opposition to him and convince him of sin, as Christ did with me and still does each day."[6] With these basic acknowledgments we can start the conversation. The process of repression is noticeable every-

[6] J. H. Bavinck, *An Introduction to the Science of Missions*. Tr. by David H. Freeman. Philadelphia: Presbyterian and Reformed, 1960, p. 242.

where in the history of religion. Man seeks God and at the
same time flees from Him; man tries to get to know God, but
at the same time he is busy obscuring the image he receives
of God's everlasting power and deity. Fear is the deepest
cause of this. In his heart of hearts man has a vague sense
that he is trying to fool God, and that he is guilty before God.
Through this fear and this feeling of guilt he represses the
image of God and replaces it by his own ideas. Man is, as
Calvin said in his *Institutes,* a *fabrica idolorum.*

It seems to me that this can best be illustrated by the meaning of the Kingdom. The Kingdom of God means the harmonious order of all creatures in one great relation, so that
every creature has its own place and dutifully fulfills its own
function in the whole, under the loving rule of God Himself.
With regard to man it means that he is both a particle in the
cosmos and at the same time more than that. He is God's
deputy; he has a very special vocation. He is the object of
God's activity and at the same time a fellow subject, God's
fellow worker. This implies a marked responsibility. He is a
person, because God addresses him with *you.* He may rule
everything that is created, because God has entrusted it to
him, but in ruling he remains God's servant all the time. The
one thing man is not allowed to do is to leave his appointed
place and to make himself a new center and ignore God. And
man is always apt to do this very thing. Through his distorted idea of reality his whole image of the cosmos and of
God is distorted. Man lives in a world full of illusions.

In these chapters we have given different illustrations. It
is not always easy to pinpoint the activity of repression and
substitution, but we can at least make the following observations.

(1) It seems to me that a great temptation is inherent in
what we have called "the sense of cosmic relationship." Of
course it is true that man belongs to the great cosmic community and that he is an integral part of it, but as soon as man

regards this as the heart of his religious life and thought, he represses something, namely, his deputyship, which is at the same time his responsibility. We have seen that man, belonging as he does to modern, scientific civilization, tends to have what we have called the "platform idea." Modern man imagines himself to be standing on a platform in the world, and is in danger of forgetting that he, too, is merely a creature and thereby subject to God's rule. But in the different religions of the world we see again and again the desire of man to reduce himself to a thing and to drown himself in the great ocean of the cosmic relations.

(2) In this connection we must remark that this tendency to reduce oneself to a thing is at the same time often attended by a certain over-boldness, which manifests itself in the attempt to take the divine powers supposedly lodging in oneself and in this world into one's own hands. We see in the magic acts that occupy such a large place in all religions a trace of the desire to interfere coercively in the occult phenomena. Man, an insignificant thing in the cosmos, at the same time imagines himself to be a god. He manipulates magical objects or formulas, and thus tries to establish his own place in the cosmos.

A more or less materialistic design lies at the root of all religious ritual which aims at material prosperity and happiness. All of life is marked by religious practices, but they are all motivated by the pursuit of earthly prosperity. God and his world are constantly regarded, and used, as a means to an end.

The great vision of the Kingdom which sees God as the center of everything, and understands God's intent with everything, is obscured time and again. Then man sees the Kingdom as the cosmic community from which God is either removed, or entirely drawn into it and no longer really different from it. But all this disrupts man's situation; he no longer occupies the place he is meant to occupy.

(3) When we discussed the norm, we came to the conclusion that all religions have realized that man is confronted with divine norms, which govern him and demand obedience. We have noticed, however, that here, too, man's repression has been very active. Man felt that the norm is inherent in the cosmos. It is the cosmic order which governs man as long as he is in the cosmos. But at certain times of the year, when a new period begins, and man returns to the era before the origin of the world, the norm does not count. Ascetics, mystics, and divine heroes are not subject to it either. So there are areas where the norm does not hold absolute sway, and consequently sin need not always be taken seriously. True, sin is an offense against the social and cosmic order and hence automatically brings along all kinds of suffering, but it is not guilt in the full sense of the word. Sin simply means being subject to the degrading powers of this world of illusions; it means being subject to *samsara,* which in essence is *avidya,* ignorance. It is a great impediment on the way to salvation, but it is not opposition against God; it is not guilt.

This does not mean, however, that the idea of guilt is nowhere found in the non-Christian religions. There, too, we find penitential psalms, songs in which sin is confessed and grace is implored. These songs sometimes show traces of self-excuse, but it is not fair to say that they all ring untrue. We may say that by the grace of God repression and substitution do not always succeed. Time and again we notice things in the history of religion which show that God has really concerned Himself with these people.

(4) Regarding the question of whether man is the author of his life or the victim of outside powers, we notice characteristic hesitation in the different religions. We have seen how Islam struggled with this problem, and how the Hindu idea of *karma* actually tries to unite the aspects of both impotence and moral appeal. But it always appears that at decisive moments, when man is confronted with great disaster, or when he

discovers that he has made a mess of things, the thought enters his mind that he is first of all a victim, and that his life is never entirely his act. The Bible shows that Adam already blamed his sin on others; and the tendency to hide behind others, behind circumstances, behind the world God made, is today still as great. This again is *repression.* It takes a great deal of courage daily to kneel down before God and honestly and sincerely confess one's sins. But such confession alone is the way to the Kingdom, for it puts man in the place in which God had once put him.

(5) Salvation. We have seen that man has always dreamt of redemption. Man nowhere accepts reality as it presents itself to him. Every man in primitive religion tries to elevate reality to a higher, sacramental, order through his rites. The cry for redemption resounds like a moving *miserere* through all the ages of history.

As soon as we ask what man means by redemption, we at once encounter repression again. In most instances religious man regarded redemption as deliverance from impotence, from misery, from illness and need, from ignorance, from *samsara,* from being bound to the dust. Although this desire may be very essential and understandable, it does not touch the root of the matter as it is seen in the light of God's Kingdom. How do we find a merciful God? In Him alone, and through the right attitude to Him, all other things are and become right. All things in creation approach each other; they "hear" each other, as the prophet Hosea has said. When the Bible speaks of salvation, it always does so in a cosmic sense. It is never concerned with man's individual redemption, not even with that of the human race as a whole. The Bible always includes all of the universe in God's act of salvation through Jesus Christ. All things are gathered together in Him. There will be a new heaven and a new earth where God will be all in all. But this salvation is God's work alone. He does it, although in such a way that He includes man in His activity from the very beginning. God does it through Jesus Christ. Therefore the message concerning Christ is the root of the biblical revelation.

(6) And finally, regarding man's view of God Himself, we have seen that he struggles with all kinds of hesitations. Is God the High God, the Supreme Being, who travels to a far, inaccessible land? Or is He the mysterious, supernatural power that resides in things and in man himself as well? Is He a "he," or a "she," or an "it"? What must we imagine Him to be? We see in the history of religion that man has always struggled with these problems. In masochistic passion he sometimes liked to be tortured and humiliated by a fearful God. He tried to find God's image in the world round about him, and saw at the moment he discovered the divine powers in the world that he himself, as a microcosmos, was part of these powers. Man has often played with his gods and broken their statues when it was obvious that they did not listen to his wishes. Man has thought that God was like the silent, impersonal, primeval ocean, or like a great fire in which we, like sparks, fly up for a moment only to fall back again when our existence comes to an end. But in all these ideas about God, important truths are somehow repressed. God is different, totally different, from the way we human beings have imagined Him in our religious fantasies. In Jesus Christ alone, the *Logos,* the Word, we hear His voice and see His image.

(7) This must be the witness of the Church when it comes into contact with other religions. It is a witness that must be given without any pride. And it is not merely the message of the Western nations to those of other parts of the world. It is God's message to all of us, without distinction of race and people.

This message concerns God's Kingdom, God Himself, and His world, in which we have a place. It concerns Jesus Christ, the Savior, on whose suffering, death, and resurrection the future of the Kingdom is founded. The message concerning the

Kingdom is to a certain extent an unmasking — it reveals the very deep processes of repression and substitution and makes us ashamed of what we have done with God. This message is revealing, as it shows what goes on in man and in the world, and what God's intention is for all things, and for man, too, His deputy on earth. This message cannot wrap itself in philosophical arguments, it cannot "prove" anything, it cannot be "logical" in every respect. It is poor and small in the world, like that of Paul when he brought it to the world of his day "not with excellency of speech or of wisdom" (I Cor. 2:1). This message has only one powerful weapon, namely, that its messengers know that if they bring it obediently and honestly, trusting in God's help and in His Spirit, it will somehow touch the heart of man. For no matter how much man in his wickedness has repressed God's truth, when the word of the gospel comes to him, something deep within his heart may be touched. Then the engines of repression are stopped, as it were, and only then he sees clearly who he himself is, and who his God is, and what the Kingdom is for which God intended him. And could this not be what the Bible calls "regeneration," the regeneration of the individual man as a sign of the regeneration of the whole cosmos?